Diary of a
Soccer Dad

Focusing on Life Lessons
in Youth Sports

This is definitely about Sports with Friends!

Kent Malmros

Tinkerati LLC

To my daughters,
Kendall and Hayden Malmros

Table of Contents

Acknowledgements

This book has been years in the making. I was once a sports journalist, who transitioned into the business world and left writing behind. Sort of. The itch remained, and I found various ways to scratch it, sketching out half-baked projects over the years. Those projects were fun and somewhat fulfilling. But they never felt like the work that I was meant to do.

Without walking you through my career progression, it became clear several years ago that I wanted to write business books. I mulled over various concepts, but never quite found the ability to stick with them. The aspiration did not translate to execution.

Then a series of events strung together, finally propelling me into a consistent routine required to persist through the Seth Godin *dip*, and ultimately *ship*.

It started innocuously enough. Sitting in the waiting room of my daughter's dance studio, I began talking to one of the staff members. I had spoken with Lois Scott before. But this conversation was different. We dug into my career and hers, our various backgrounds and more. It was a fantastic conversation that came with an unexpected closing dialogue.

"Are you a writer?" Lois said to me. "Because you sound like a person who has something important to say."

I explained to her that, while I had been *trying* to write, I hadn't really found my voice. Lois simply encouraged me to do it. No need to look for the perfect idea, she said. My voice would produce something worth reading. Indeed, her unexpected push that day provided newfound confidence that translated into momentum.

To be sure, that wasn't enough. But the universe began paving a path to productivity for me. Out of the blue, my trusted colleague and dear friend, Laura Wilson, asked me to participate in a Master Mind group with her and another former colleague, David Noonan. She was looking for a creative support system, and without knowing my growing ambitions, thought I'd be interested and willing. This group took the form of a weekly call – thirty minutes every Friday, at the outset. It gave me permission to make time for my writer-self. It also gave me the motivation to do the work. After all, you can't show up to talk about projects on which you're not actually working. Right?

I am grateful to our weekly group calls. I am more grateful for Laura's friendship, encouragement and guidance on this project. As a colleague, Laura believed in me. After we stopped working together, she continued to believe in me. She encouraged me to write, also suggesting I had something to say. Most specifically, though, Laura shaped what this book became. When I started *Diary of a Soccer Dad*, it was called *Soccer Dad CEO*. I aspired to write a business book neatly tucked inside a book about my experiences as a soccer dad. As I wrote, it was clear that I was telling a different story, I just wasn't sure what that story was or how I should pivot. Needing an unbiased and trusted opinion, I turned to Laura.

She read the pages I gave her and delivered a thoughtful and well-crafted opinion on the value contained herein. *Diary of a Soccer Dad* was born on the heels of a thirty-minute conversation, and the first draft basically wrote itself in fits and starts during the weeks that ensued.

There are many people that helped this book evolve thereafter. Jake Nesteruk read with perspective I was seeking. Russ Womack provided guidance on a few levels. Steve Castellano's keen eye was invaluable. Brian Brossman provided creative visualization for the cover art. As did Anthony "TJ" Vaught.

Of course, there are indirect acknowledgements that need to be made as well. Jon Acuff for giving the world *Finish* so I could read and apply it. Then for having Brian Koppelman as a guest on his first podcast, so I could discover Brian's podcast, *The Moment*. Both have unknowingly been an invaluable source of continued encouragement and guidance on this creative journey.

Patricia Liddie was the first teacher who made me believe I could write. No words can express how important it was for me to spend a year in her classroom. Thank you.

My parents always told me I could be anything I wanted. Even a ballet dancer. Mark and Debbie Malmros will certainly prefer that I chose this type of art.

Kendall and Hayden, my beautiful, brilliant, fun, passionate and driven daughters inspire me every day to be a better parent. And, also, to share my insights so that our collective journey may help others.

Finally, my wife Cindy. We met when I dreamt of being a writer. As life took us in other directions, I felt I had abandoned writing. She always knew it was temporary. Even as I did other things, pursued other careers and paid bills in other ways, *she told people I was a writer* when they asked the standard question, "what does your husband do?"

In truth, there's no such thing as *Diary of a Soccer Dad* without the *encouragement of a soccer mom*. She has also told me, always, I've had something to say that others would want to hear. This book would not exist without her, in so many different ways. I often tell people that, no matter how much you try to ask a partner about their philosophies on parenting, it's still a guess. The best you can do is try to align on core values and hope they ultimately apply to the parenting styles you assume when kids finally arrive. I am so fortunate that Cindy and I shared those values from the day we met. When Kendall and Hayden were born, everything we thought we knew changed. Except those core values. We modified our behavior to accommodate the world but retained alignment to those values.

In almost every way, that's what this book is about. Cindy and I have walked blindly down the road of sports parenthood, guided by the light of our values. I believe we are headed in the right direction and towards the right destination. I wanted to share that journey with you.

I thank her for taking it with me and letting me tell you about it.

Introduction:
Hiding on the Sidelines

August 20th

Dear Diary,
This parenting thing… it's really, really hard. Particularly when you're trying to help your kids make good decisions as they walk through a world filled with candy-colored landmines. It seems so sweet and innocent, even fun. But taking a bite can be devastating.

That's how participating in youth sports feels now. Kendall started playing soccer with her blonde ponytail bobbing endlessly on top of an oversized purple jersey, simultaneously scared and smiling. Well, that's sort of a lie. When she first *started playing, there was only fear. She wouldn't even run up-and-down the field with the other mob of kids furiously kicking up dust but missing the ball. We begged her just to stand out there and give it a shot. Reluctantly, she did. Then, eventually, she started to participate.*

After that, it was all smiles.

She even got good. And that's when she started having more fun. As a five-year-old, she scored eleven goals in one game! There were no goalkeepers, true. But it was still clear she had a knack for the sport. And her abilities took off from there. Kendall started playing on better teams and doing well. Which led her to try out for (and make) even better teams where she could compete at a very high level.
Four short years after that eleven-goal outbreak, our life became consumed by soccer. That's the point at which it all started to get very confusing.

The candy shell completely melted away and all that remained were the

1

landmines. The results have been, well, short of catastrophic, but still damaging at times.

Not all the time. There are still incredible moments, to be sure. See what I mean? Confusing! It's truly hard to understand how we got here.

But here's the thing. This is not acceptable. There has to be a better way. How can we make youth sports truly worthwhile, like we all know it can be? I'm sick of hiding on the sidelines waiting for the next landmine to go off.

Any advice? Thanks in advance.

Sincerely,
Kent (aka, Soccer Dad)

The origin
The idea for this book was prompted by several concurrent happenings, starting with a short Twitter conversation. *Athletic specialization occurs too early*, was the general tone of the tweet I read. That's a well-documented debate, and one worth explicitly avoiding in these pages (though the concepts are related to some of our themes as well). But it served as the beginning of a broader dialogue regarding the general state of youth sports.

Youth sports has become an enormous business, unquestionably. In the last two decades, seasonal sports have become a thing of the past. It's possible for children to play soccer, baseball, basketball, lacrosse and pretty much any other sport twelve months a year, without a break. All with mounting costs and diminishing free time.

This has created an environment of fierce competition. One that has fostered that trend of early specialization – ten-year old kids focused exclusively on one sport – for fear of "falling behind" their counterparts. Surely, a girl has no chance of earning college scholarships if she isn't the best player on her eleven-year old soccer team, right? Right!

Wrong. Profoundly wrong. The research says otherwise. For anyone seeking perspective on the current climate surrounding youth sports, *Changing the Game* is recommended reading. John O'Sullivan equips you with the perspective and tools to ensure that youth sports participation is a healthy experience for your children and family. [1] If you buy the book and have children playing sports with any level of dedication, read it. Then read it again. And give it to everyone you know.

---

[1] O'Sullivan, John. *Changing the Game: The Parent's Guide to Raising Happy, High Performing Athletes, and Giving Youth Sports Back to our Kids* (New York: Morgan James Publishing, 2014)

Come to think of it, *if you want your child* to become a dedicated athlete, even if she hasn't yet reached that level, have your child also read it. Twice.

Books like *Changing the Game* have informed a strong but clear minority of sports parents. The Twitter conversation referenced above included such enlightened voices. But, the content of that conversation was different than O'Sullivan's effort to maximize experiences on the field. Instead of focusing on how to ensure your child becomes her best player self, the debate quickly branched into all the other positive attributes associated with youth sports. The attributes are often perceived as tangential, not the primary impacts of participation.

- *I'd prefer my children spend three hours working hard and getting fit than sitting in front of a screen playing video games.*

- *Playing sports teaches my kids how to work hard, learn discipline and stay dedicated in a way nothing else can.*

- *It's worth every penny for my children to understand teamwork and grittiness, even if they only play a few years.*

Wide-ranging and positive, the responses outlined the true advantages of offering athletics to our children. It was inspiring. There were life lessons to be gained in sports that had nothing to do with winning. It was the beginning of a blueprint. But it was also imperfect in a way that virtually all conversations on this topic are incomplete. There are so many additional aspects to explore – more lessons that couldn't possibly be covered in 140-character exchanges.

The topic deserved its own study and focus.

The evolution

That realization prompted a personal exercise to understand how we articulate the very best value associated with our children's efforts.

Parents are amazed by their children, and I'm no exception. When I started this project, my two daughters, Kendall and Hayden, had achieved more at eleven and nine, respectively, in pursuit of their passions than I ever did. Granted, the world changed dramatically over the course of two-ish decades between the end of my childhood and the beginning of theirs. That reality presents both opportunities and challenges for the next generation of dreamers. But, their varied accomplishments are still miraculous.

There's bias in the paragraph above. That's what parents do, and we will discuss how to approach that bias later. But, for now, humor me and let me outline it for you anyway; you can form your own opinion.

Kendall is a fantastic athlete. By just after her eleventh birthday, she had already progressed from local, intramural soccer to the top team in her age group at one of the top-ranked girls' soccer clubs in the country – Players Development Academy (PDA) in Zarephath, New Jersey. It wasn't an easy journey (and, at the time I'm writing this, some struggles continue) because Kendall was a perpetual underdog for various reasons. She was both smaller than other girls and a late-bloomer. Meaning that, in addition to being a bit shorter than everyone, she was a touch behind in the muscle department.

Kendall is also wired a bit differently than many other kids. She's incredibly cerebral. It's certainly an advantage in the classroom – Kendall is a top student and voracious reader with an interest in robotics – but not always on the soccer field as a young girl. In youth sports, the most physically mature and aggressive often progress the fastest. They push people around and run as fast as they can.

Meanwhile, Kendall thinks the game when she doesn't need to. She understands tactics when they aren't necessarily obvious.

Her areas for development are often about risk, aggression, physicality, and creativity. Those are the lessons most often reinforced with her coming off the field or during our drive home from practice, as we approached "being a sports parent" in the most typical way.

Hayden, on the other hand, is the artist. Her weekly schedule includes twelve hours of dance class – ballet, tap, jazz, lyrical, and modern – and participation on four different competition teams. When it's time to perform, no audience is too big, and no light is too bright. When dance class is over, Hayden comes home and dances for another hour (maybe two).

Passion has carried her beyond the achievement level of many peers. Frequently, she is front-and-center in group formations for recital performances. Hayden is often the youngest in her class. Sometimes, in fact, she feels underappreciated for her skill, even among kids five years her senior.

We often work with her on setting appropriate, self-driven expectations. Lessons include navigating the nuances of being a teammate, and setting personal goals balanced against team goals.

Great experiences, right? For the most part, I understood how rich and fulfilling these opportunities were for Kendall and Hayden as they pursued them during the first few years. Yet, with each passing week, as the commitment increased, the environments continued to focus more on results. Outcomes. Accomplishment. And it started to feel somewhat confusing, honestly. What were they chasing?

It became hard to answer that question in a way that was grounded in both the present and future and built on a solid foundation of data-driven reality.

That's when we decided it was time to adjust perspective. Interestingly, as this was happening for me, it was also happening for Kendall. We just didn't realize it yet.

Youth activities have become such a large commitment that families need to take a step back and evaluate what every member is gaining from holistic participation. *Jake is going to learn teamwork, that's fantastic!* What's in it for everyone else? Is it enough to justify the effort? Shouldn't Jake be learning more than teamwork if he's spending twelve hours a week dedicated to baseball?

We forget to ask the following question daily: are there *more critical life lessons* we can all glean from our children's activities? I started to ask that question, constantly. The experience of asking and answering it was truly transformative.

The realization
It's important to note that I spent most of my time helping with the family soccer schedule. Not for the expected reason – there's not a male sports bias here. It's more an experiential issue. Dance preparation often requires bunning hair and applying makeup. My wife has years of experience in both areas and when it's time to divide and conquer, she's much more likely to conquer hair and makeup. However, I have become proficient at bunning Hayden's hair. Just wanted to make that clear.

With that said, my self-evaluation started on the sidelines of the soccer field because I spent more time there; most recently, hiding on the sidelines.

When Kendall first started playing soccer, I was an enthusiastic and active participant. Watching her sessions, my objective was to understand how she was being instructed and help reinforce the nuances of technical work, so I could try to help her improve soccer skills.

7

At games, I fell into the common trap of parent-coaching. Not obnoxiously, but enough.

In the spring of 2016, Kendall tried out for, and was offered a spot at Players Development Academy (PDA). At that very moment, it became clear that we couldn't help her *with soccer*. Yes, she was only nine when tryouts started, and ten by the time she made the team. But she was playing at a level well above anything we could understand. It was at that point that we decided to start hiding on the sidelines. We became quiet at practice and quiet about her performance – choosing instead to loudly cheer on her team and teammates.

Still we continued to reinforce the critical lessons that came with playing sports. Or at least those we thought were important. In hindsight, we were doing it wrong, if not the best we could. She was good enough to play at a very high level, so we kept urging her to work hard, compete, and be aggressive.

As we were encouraging her to pursue her soccer dreams, it was also clear two years after joining PDA that soccer had lost its luster. The focus on development felt like it had vanished, and the focus on fun had long since disappeared. Kendall was actively questioning what she was getting out of a pursuit from which she had spent so much of her young life.

So was I.

If we were both trying to understand the value of soccer – and youth activities more broadly – some real questions needed to be asked. *I can help Kendall and her passion for soccer.* Just in a different way.

And soccer could help me rediscover some of the key lessons life has to offer. As I considered what those lessons were, I actually found they were hiding plainly in front of me on a soccer field and could make them the focus of Kendall's youth sports experience. That's what this book is about.

The application for Kendall

Diary of a Soccer Dad will walk you through the lessons I began to identify as part of our recommitment to youth sports. It became apparent that pursuing excellence on the field was far less important than achieving personal growth off the field.

This book will outline the life lessons I actively identified and cultivated (and still cultivate) for Kendall as our relationship with youth soccer evolved.

… It started as an effort to be a better soccer parent.
… It continued as an effort to salvage Kendall's participation in sports.
… It ended as a guide to get the most value out of youth sports, no matter how long a child plays, or at what level.

Why this book?

This book is about tools. Tools that remind us of critical life lessons found on the soccer field, and everywhere for that matter. Each chapter contains one idea that I observed and then reinforced as a soccer dad, as well as an example (or multiple examples) of how I applied that idea to maximize Kendall's time on a soccer field.

Ultimately, these tools inspired me to be a better sports parent, dad and person. I hope they inspire you to apply lessons learned as a parent, friend, spouse or family member to your pursuits as well.

One last thought

This book is not about how to manage your children's athletic (or other activity-based) performance. Other people offer much greater expertise in that area.

However, there's no doubt that my shift in perspective has created greater balance and health around my daughters' pursuit of excellence. The more I focused on learning from them, the less time I spent *worried* about their relative "accomplishments" in dance or soccer.

Why? Because, a full life is developed from a growth mindset, not a fixed mindset. It's virtually impossible for a parent to overemphasize the outcome of any given practice or game if, instead, they are thinking about how to better emphasize related life goals that matter more.

Thinking this way, my relationship with my daughters and their passions is healthier. I hope you achieve the same result.

Chapter Zero:
How to Use This Book

August 21st

Dear Diary,

I was thinking about yesterday's entry and I've made a decision. The answers are actually right in front of me, and part of my experiences with youth sports. I played baseball my whole life, and when I take a step back, it's so clear to me how the countless hours I spent on a baseball field have shaped the person I've become.

That recognition only happened in hindsight, of course. So, I don't expect Kendall to figure it out herself.

But it's perplexing that parents (including me!) can lose sight of the real-life lessons embedded in youth sports participation. Really, what's wrong with all of us?

It's time to take back control of the situation. I'm going to start journaling the lessons we're supposed to help our kids learn through their sports experiences. And, frankly, it will probably help me re-learn and apply those very same lessons to my own life along the way.

There are life lessons everywhere, and youth sport is no exception. You just have to pay attention to them. That's exactly what I intend to do.

Sincerely,
Kent (aka, Soccer Dad)

The journal entries

For starters, let's be direct. These diary and journal entries are fake. Unfortunately, foresight didn't suggest that a book was needed to guide or navigate the rocky road of parenting an athlete. But these are the entries that should have been written along the way. So, we're using them to introduce the concepts addressed in each chapter.

There are lessons in the fictionalized journal entries, sure. But we expand on them in great detail, talking about the key nuanced lessons you can help your children learn during their time committed to youth sports. Here's a hint: they are not about scoring as many goals on the soccer field as possible or becoming the world's angriest winner.

Yes, some are directly related to what your child does on the field. But they are also related to the approach you and your child take while participating overall.

It's about parents and children

That's right, you and your child. Not just your child. Being an appropriate participant in your child's athletic development can teach or re-teach you key life lessons as well. You just have to be open to it. Once you're open to it, you can help them learn those lessons through their participation in sports.

There's an added benefit, as well. The more you focus on improving yourself as a sports parent, the less energy you spend pressuring your child to perform, improve or otherwise focus on performance-based outcomes.

Yes, we are saying upfront those are the wrong things. If you picked up this book expecting a secret formula to turn your daughter into the next star of the United States Women's National Team, close it now and put it down. Wait! Before you close the book, think of someone that isn't a crazy sports parent and give it to them. They may appreciate what we have to say.

If you are that crazy parent, and you're still here, maybe you recognize it's time to change. Good, we can help. Keep reading.

The lessons
This book is entirely dedicated to helping you and your child learn life lessons from sports. Period. The content is based on personal experience and a touch of additional research.

There are seventeen lessons, divided into four sections:

1. *Getting to the Field: Supporting the Journey*
2. *On the Field: Impacting How the Game Is Played*
3. *Coming off the Field: Focus on Outcomes and Interpretation*
4. *Wrapping Up: Applying the Concepts and Looking for More*

The sections are designed to call out specific aspects of the daily parent/child sports experience and attach a primary lesson to each. It's easy to look at your days and see that the actions are simple – you drive your child to practice or a game, they participate and then you drive them home.

Yet, in those simple actions, we embed any number of situational behaviors that shape our relationship with that experience, and your child's relationship with that experience. What you choose to do with those simple actions, and the related behaviors, can dramatically impact the outcomes of your child's time as a young athlete and their evolution as a person.

Heavy stuff, right? It's true. You may dedicate more time to participating in youth sports than anything in their lives except for sleep and school. And for some, the devotion to sports may well exceed the time spent on academic pursuits. We're not here to judge whether that's the right thing to do. If your child is having fun and learning key life lessons, keep spending the time. Just make it count.

One chapter at a time

Consider the larger lessons embedded throughout this book. But, don't let them overwhelm you. Each chapter is based on anecdotes that ground the behaviors and lessons in specific experiences related to the daily grind of youth sports participation.

Feel free to read them and apply them one at a time. Most likely, you'll be in the car on the way to practice two or three times a week. If you explore one behavior at a time, you'll work your way through this book in under two months. That's a small window of time to adjust your approach to something that may occupy the next several years of your life.

Recommended actions have been provided at the end of each section. These have been consolidated into an "actions" section at the back of the book. It should provide a reference that you can utilize when and as needed. Each action is relatively simple. But, like any habit, you can't internalize them all at once. Choose one or two per week and put them to work. By the time you've implemented ten or more, you will see a dramatic impact in how you are leveraging one critical part of your life for another.

When working through an action, make sure that life lessons takes priority over examining your child's simple performance. In other words, her willingness to make mistakes is more important than whether or not she scored a goal. Pay attention to the outcomes and note any personal adjustments you need to make.

Explore how you can apply (or reapply) the same lessons to your own life at work, home or beyond. This book focuses on the key youth sports lessons that extend off the field and provide a rich playground for long-term growth. If the ideas are good enough for your child, they're good enough for you. Modelling them in your own life will make them more impactful in your child's. Embrace and practice them to see an improvement in your own outlook.

I hope this enriches your life the same way the process enriched ours.

Part One:
Getting to the Field

(Supporting the Journey)

Chapter One:
Fun First

Dear Diary,
The season has just started, and it already feels like it's been dragging on forever. Kendall never smiles anymore. It doesn't make sense. She used to LOVE playing soccer. She would get excited about practice and games. She wanted to train more with other coaches. Then she'd come home and juggle her soccer ball. The pursuit was fun. The work was fun. It was all fun!

Now she seems unhappy on the way to practice. And on the way home from practice. She never touches a soccer ball at home. She doesn't want to watch games. I don't get it.

It makes me sad to think that something she once loved has become such a chore. I think she may quit playing altogether if she can't find a way to enjoy it again in the future.

What do I do? How do we rediscover the fun?

This seems important and like the foundation of youth sports, we need to figure it out.

Sincerely,
Kent (aka, Soccer Dad)

Games are fun, right?

There is only one reason to begin playing sports – for fun. Somehow, shortly thereafter, the objective changes. Naturally, kids become competitive. And for some, that's another way they have fun. If your child competes enough and shows an aptitude for sports, the pull to become a "star" will arise. That's partly because sports have become a big business, with big opportunity attached.

Consider that a college scholarship can save families over $100,000, $200,000 or more in cash or debt. Then you may understand why so many get caught up in a short-sighted view and invest so much in the "hope" of athletic achievement. That pursuit starts by middle school (if not earlier). If your daughter began playing soccer at seven and begins chasing college dreams (or more) by twelve, then only five years of sports is truly played for fun. Most likely, between ages ten and twelve, it may become clear that your daughter is good enough (or not) to consider that collegiate dream. In that case, the "fun" period of play includes jumping from one club to a better club to ensure the level of play encourages growth.

That's to say nothing of the countless additional hours of individual or group training required to compete at the highest levels. But we'll get back to that momentarily.

Does that sound fun?

What is fun?

It is critical to remind yourself why you introduced sports to your children in the first place. Because it's fun!

- Running around without care is fun!
- Competing with other kids is fun!
- Learning a new skill is fun!
- Perfecting that skill is really fun!
- Winning is fun!

- Losing isn't fun...
- But building camaraderie with your teammates in pursuit of a win is fun!
- Wearing cool gear is fun!
- Traveling to new places, for games, is fun!

There are so many reasons to begin playing sports that it's a wonder some people don't participate. It can be a rich, character-building experience, but it should *be* fun. And it should *stay* fun.

This book is about learning life lessons through sports. The first lesson is to make sure sports start and remain fun because fun is important. Without fun, your child won't play sports long enough to learn the other life lessons in this book.

Kendall's joy
Kendall fell into the category described above quickly – it was clear she had an aptitude for soccer, some natural talent, and a voracious appetite to improve.

At the outset, that *was* the fun part for her. She enjoyed training, so she wanted to find her way to extra sessions. Kendall is a perfectionist, so she loved the process of improving and found motivation in every small success. As Jeff Haden argues in his book *The Motivation Myth*, we don't become motivated in a moment of grand inspiration, but rather through small, incremental successes that build and sustain enthusiasm.[2]

That's how it worked for Kendall. Sure, she scored some goals as an athletic five-year old. But she loved learning how to pass correctly. How to shoot correctly. How to execute various dribbling moves. Challenging herself to perfect technical skills such as dribbling with every part of her foot, a pull-back or scissor was exhilarating. Every

[2] Haden, Jeff. *The Motivation Myth: How High Achievers Really Set Themselves Up to Win* (New York: Portfolio, 2018)

time she touched a ball, there was joy. There was motivation to do more. When she perfected a new technique, happiness abounded.

Technical prowess naturally led to better performance on the field, which in turn led to opportunities with better teams. The only problem with such a progression was that better teams demanded even more. By the time she was ten, Kendall was training five or six days each week at first for the joy of improvement, but then just to keep up with (or try to stay ahead of) the talent-level on her now elevated teams. What was once fun had become a *job*.

Finding time to play other sports became more challenging. It was possible to keep them in the schedule, but impossible to commit to any of them fully. Weekends were eaten up by games, tournaments or clinics.

The fun associated with soccer became tougher and tougher to find.

Sure, some kids are so driven at a young age that this level of commitment is fun for them. Truthfully, that is both abnormal and unlikely to be healthy for their overall development. A parent of Kendall's one teammate bragged that her daughter loved soccer so much, she had played in three tournaments – eleven games – over the course of a two-day weekend. Very few kids have that much fun playing soccer, and it was impossible to believe she wasn't influenced by her parents, who desperately wanted her to be a star. Even if it was that player's choice, parents should consider whether to intervene and limit that level of participation. They need to ask if playing that much over a short period of time is appropriate. Or even fun. What's the purpose?

Losing fun
There is one item missing from the list above that leads to fun. New experiences. There is no doubt that experiencing new, unknown and unexpected things can be incredibly fun. It's one of the unique

elements of playing sports – every event is a real-life drama, waiting to unfold before your daughter's eyes. As an athlete, she gets to be part of it.

As Kendall chased better competition and ambitious goals, truly new experiences became harder to find. In the spring of 2017, this was exactly the trap we had fallen into. In hindsight, it was completely understandable. The previous eighteen months had been a non-stop grind.

In the winter of 2015-2016, Kendall made it her goal to try out for and make PDA. While she had demonstrated talent and production with her previous teams, we talked about what it would take to break into the club. Yes, her season at a local club had just ended, but she would need to train diligently to give herself the best chance of receiving an offer. Regular group training was scheduled, as well as private sessions with a preferred trainer. She took five days off between December and May, and she was offered a spot on one of two teams in her age group at PDA. As an outsider, that was fantastic. A great place to start her journey at the club.

Practices started within a few weeks, and the team played together in three tournaments over the summer as well. Two weeks off gave way to a fall schedule… and before we knew it, a winter schedule and spring schedule brought us right back to tryouts twelve months later. It went by in a flash. There was hardly any time to stop and reflect on what was going on – good or bad. As part of the club, she was training with the same intensity she had the previous year. By the end of May, Kendall found out that she would be moving to the other team in her age group, which competed at an even higher level.

And the cycle began almost immediately once again. Without a break. By the middle of her second fall season at PDA, it was clear that Kendall was simply exhausted. Physically. Mentally. Emotionally.

Most importantly, she just didn't seem to be having fun.

Reclaiming fun

As parents, you struggle in these moments. To get to this point, you've encouraged, sacrificed, pushed, pulled, supported, and consoled. No matter how much the focus has been on achievement, there are other forces at play of which you never want to lose sight.

But...fun?!? Isn't that what this is all about? Or what it was supposed to be about? Particularly at a young age.

Kendall had lost sight of fun. She needed to regain it. The natural inclination would have been to focus on rest. Maybe a clear mind and healthy body would be more fun. That was one perspective. It was, certainly, a point of view offered by close friends.

There was rest on the horizon, however. A few weeks off before fall practice started with her club, and a week vacation to South Carolina in between. Time off, fully immersed in beach living or reading, would certainly be fun. *But it wouldn't make soccer fun.*

So, we went a different route. We suggested *more* soccer options to Kendall, but instead of investing more time in her team, we recommended a return to other things that made soccer fun for her. New experiences, with new people and new challenges. She had once loved, but now lost, the newness of it all. She still loved soccer, but also loved the adventures soccer brought her. And those had gone missing.

We presented a few camps and clinics that would take her outside the environment created by her club. Kendall eventually decided she would enjoy attending a local college ID camp. If you're not familiar with ID camps, they are designed to expose athletes to college programs and coaches that interest them – ID stands for identification. In turn, the colleges get to scout players that may later be invited to their program.

It sounds like another pressure-packed situation. But, in reality, there was no pressure on Kendall.

At eleven, as a rising sixth grader, Kendall was in the youngest age group allowed at the camp. With the college recruitment process still a few years away, that wasn't her purpose for the three-day event. Instead, she was there to see new things and meet new people. It gave her a chance to return to the fun things associated with soccer.

She got to spend two nights sleeping in a college dorm, a new experience. It exposed her to dining hall food – dry chicken isn't so good, but unlimited fries and ice cream caught her attention. It was fun to make choices!

Brushing her teeth and showering regularly had been a constant struggle as well. But when it was her responsibility – she had to choose when and how long to shower – it became sort of cool. Mom and dad weren't telling her if she had to wash her hair, so she chose to do it because, well, she realized clean hair was kind of good after eight hours of sweating in ninety-degree weather.

Independence was fun, and soccer was giving her that.

Kendall met new friends from all over the country – quickly endearing herself to a girl from Connecticut and twins from South Carolina, among others.

There were new coaches from whom to learn, new girls against whom she could compete, new fields on which she could play.

While she was at camp, the nighttime phone debriefs consisted of very little soccer conversation. Instead, Kendall talked about all those other life experiences that were making her smile. She was definitely improving her soccer skills. But, mostly, she was having fun.

Kendall returned from camp with a new-found confidence. She had stories that required telling, so she was immensely more talkative. Somewhere in those stories, a rich and sharp sense of humor was further unlocked. Laughter echoed through the house at previously unprecedented rates. In short, this soccer experience had again delivered on its original promise to her – providing new and different experiences that were fun.

The combination of those factors made her undoubtedly a better soccer player. She exuded that confidence in different ways. Kendall, at eleven-years old, played differently than most kids her age. She was overly respectful of team concepts, whereas most of her peers were focused on individual achievement.

The result was often frustrating. She would wait for other players to appropriately pass her the ball and get her in the game. Sitting in space without a defender anywhere in sight, she was often the "safe" pass that would result in continued possession for her team. But, teammates were more focused on taking on opponents and doing fancy footwork, so they could score goals and get the glory. That often meant she would sit out in that space, open. Waiting for the ball.

Watching her on game nights at the camp, it was clear that the decision-making authority she experienced at meals (eat ice cream or don't?) and in the dorms (shower again? wash my hair?) extended to the field. When her teammates didn't get her involved, she took matters into her own hands, either changing tactical approach or (gulp) getting a bit selfish herself.

And guess what? She was having fun doing it.

The camp had successfully injected fun back into her playing experience. The takeaway was obvious – always make sure fun is part of the equation.

Reclaiming fun, part two
Sadly, the fun began to disappear again over the course of her fall U12 (under-twelve, the term for teams with athletes younger than twelve years old) season. The experiences we had constructed around her during the summer vanished into memory because that "fun" infrastructure didn't exist within her club situation.

As the fall season progressed, she felt no connection with her teammates, her coach, or the sport. Kendall once again became trapped in a cycle of all work no play.

At eleven, that's a death sentence for a sport you once loved. So, we made a difficult and unpopular decision: Kendall left PDA before the spring season started. In some people's eyes, she quit.

Keep in mind, of course, that the fall season was over. Winter training was over. But soccer is a year-round sport. By the time she left the team in February of 2018, she had already been part of the team for eight months, but still had four months left of her "commitment."

We genuinely feared she may hate soccer by June, so we erred on the side of fun. Kendall joined a team where she knew and loved the girls with whom she would play, and never looked back. It took her a bit to get acclimated to that new team – understanding her teammate's tendencies so she could maximize the outcome of her efforts. But, ultimately, she had an outstanding three months.

She smiled constantly, enjoying the company of the girls playing alongside her. She played freely, feeling like there were no consequences associated with her mistakes. She thrived because she was having fun in many different ways. Her love for soccer was different, without question, but it was salvaged.

Later in the book we'll talk about finding the right situation. It was easy for us to conclude that her final months at PDA were far from that. There are many reasons you make this determination, but whether you're having fun is most certainly one of them.

Fun first. Otherwise, all other lessons we discuss in this book are ultimately lost or not given the chance to be learned.

Seeing your extended family is fun
It's one of life's great axioms and you're sure to hear it from your parents and other adults when you're young. *Do something fun with your life*, they say. Often, though, they are talking about a career choice or other big picture decisions.

What about focusing on fun at the least obvious moments? What about making fun your mantra? There are chances every day to find the fun when it's been lost.

We've all been in this situation. The holidays come around and it's time to use our hard-earned vacation days to head to the house of a family member. When it was a shiny new tradition, you could hardly wait for the event. Anticipation built as you awaited the richness of your aunt's pie, the cunning of your uncle's humor, and the company of your cousins.

But, after time, the luster is lost. Everything about the trip feels familiar and it's difficult to get motivated to interact with family that you certainly still love, but to whom you can't really relate. You are bound to spend that time answering the same questions as the last year, hearing the same stories as last year, being asked to repeat the same stories as last year. The pie doesn't taste as good as it used to, the jokes aren't as funny, and your cousins aren't even there.

Needless to say, your level of enthusiasm runs low. Family time isn't always fun. But, if you were really opposed to it, you'd choose to do something else. So, there's still an element of either enjoyment or the aspiration to enjoy the time. And why not? It's family. You want to enjoy the time. And it's incredibly valuable time.

As the saying goes, you can't choose your family. That differentiates this example from youth sport participation. Playing soccer is and should be a choice, and one made based on enjoyment. At least initially.

The beauty of life lessons learned through playing sports, however, is that they can apply even in non-parallel scenarios. Take the concepts that Kendall learned above and apply them when you're not looking forward to seeing your extended family. When those holiday visits have lost their fun. Seriously, it works.

What aspects of the current trips are the most enjoyable? Maybe they aren't the penultimate example of fun, but they are the most fun available. Maybe the family has seen additional opportunities for fun that have not been exploited.

For example, Aunt Sally is a self-proclaimed board game addict, with dozens of titles stored in the living room closet. But, for some reason, her games remain in the closet while scheduled activities focus on re-watching old family videos instead. Suggest the board games! Make some goals and figure out how to incrementally improve your experience during a Thanksgiving trip to Aunt Sally's house.

Maybe the change was massive, or maybe it was incremental. Either way, the approach above should have allowed you to change the focus on family trips from obligatory and boring back to some level of fun. It's not enough. Revisit the exercise and improve upon it.

Selling girl scout cookies

Making fun a priority in soccer works. Making it the focus of family gatherings works. What about other activities?

For most kids, particularly early on, extracurricular activities are not limited to playing sports. There's a good chance your daughter dabbled in Girl Scouts (Brownies, Daisies, etc., depending on the level…). If so, she participated in the great American pastime of selling Girl Scout Cookies.

The Girls Scouts take immense pride in the fact that selling Girls Scout Cookies teaches its participants foundational business and life skills. [3] But it can also be an anxiety-producing, traumatizing requirement that causes many girls to leave an organization that can help them evolve in many other ways.

Why do some reach this point? Because for many, selling just isn't fun. At least the ideas of standing in front of some storefront selling or going door-to-door in your neighborhood aren't fun.

Girls don't sign up for Girls Scouts at age six thinking, "I'm going to become an extraordinary salesperson." Six-year old girls don't often sign themselves up for Girl Scouts at all, for that matter. But you get the idea. Assuming parents give their child some level say in the decision, that's not at the top of the reason list.

Instead, a young girl participates with the intention of having fun. And she might define that as socializing with friends, doing art projects, visiting parks or more. Selling cookies doesn't fit any of those paradigms.

---

[3] Lindsay Levine, "Lessons From Inside The $800 Million Girl Scout Cookie Selling Empire," *Fast Company*, February 19, 2014, https://www.fastcompany.com/3026561/lessons-from-inside-the-800-million-girl-scout-cookie-selling-empire.

But you can make it better by bringing the fun aspects of the scouting experience into focus during the selling exercise. Socializing is fun? Be sure to sell in groups. Going door-to-door isn't fun? Set up a lemonade stand for cookies at the entrance to your development. Completely averse to selling? Maybe you can partner with a six-year old sales whiz and offer to take care of marketing and fulfillment while she is closing deals.

No matter the initiative, values and life lessons develop when someone is enjoying something and just happens to be learning other stuff along the way. If your child doesn't ground everything in fun, the rest of the life lessons will be lost.

Fun Actions
Sports experiences can teach us that fun is the foundation on which all other life lessons are built. Here are five key actions that will help keep fun in focus. They apply to athletics and other activities for your kids.

1. Talk about what specifically makes a sport fun for your child. Ask what is the most fun aspect of her participation on a day-to-day basis. How can she maximize those specific elements?

2. Explore the opposite side of that equation. What are the least fun parts of sports or other activities? How can you work to minimize those?

3. Identify where your child seems to have hit a wall. Find out what fun growth opportunities may reinvigorate him. For your child-athlete, is it an experience, travel, a second sport, spiritual activity, or something else? For a student, is it extra emphasis on one subject without concern for another? More reading? Finding a tutor?

4. Integrate fun activities into routine. Fun shouldn't be a one-off situation. Organizing an event specifically built around fun can help.

5. As a parent, make sure you're having fun. Behavior is modeled and if you can't enjoy yourself, it may be hard for your child to do so. Go through the exercises above, pointed inward.

Chapter Two:
Passion and Drive

September 4th

Dear Diary,
I'm so proud of Kendall. Yep, I say that a lot. I mean, a whole lot. It really embarrasses her. Especially now that she's getting a bit older. And even more so because I'm her dad.

Back to the point. We've been talking about fun, and I think we're making the right adjustments to ensure that fun is the top priority in her soccer world. She definitely loves the game, which doesn't always seem obvious when she's not having fun. But now that we've found fun again, there's so much she can get out of it.

So back to why I'm proud of her. I'm proud of her because she works hard to improve as a soccer player. She seems to really love it. No... actually, it's not that. I mean, she does love it, but that's not what I'm seeing. She loves working at it to become better. She's passionate about it, in fact! She will focus on the details related to a particular technique and make sure she studies how to perfect them. She's driven to learn sophisticated skills that require immense coordination. Which means there's tons of practice involved. That's why I'm proud – she leverages that passion to stay driven to improve.

Passion and drive can take you places – more so than hard work. We need to talk about that, so she holds on to it. Make sense? That's our next discussion on the way to practice. I'll let you know how it goes.

Sincerely,
Kent (aka, Soccer Dad)

The beginning felt like the end

When Kendall was four, she didn't want to play soccer. As parents, we signed her up for various activities, trying to give her exposure to things she might enjoy. Soccer was one of many – basketball, dance, music and gymnastics were among the others – intended to keep her active and bring her enjoyment.

Yet, soccer terrified her. Kendall ran out onto the field as a four-year-old, and then cried when the ball and other kids all began to move. She would try to run off the field and hide behind her family standing on the sidelines.

It took coaxing and cajoling to get Kendall to simply *stay on the field.* "You don't even have to run," we'd tell her during water breaks. "Just stand out there and watch." It worked. She looked sad and fought back tears, but she did at least stay on the field.

With that in mind, it was a wonder that just five short years later, as an ambitious nine-year-old Kendall told us she wanted to try and play at PDA. Located forty-five minutes from our house, it was unquestionably one of the most reputable clubs in our region, and often ranked among the best girls' soccer clubs in the nation.

Joining the club was a tall order for an outside player like Kendall, who wasn't known there and hadn't played at that level.

That's not to say she hadn't progressed incredibly well since we convinced her to at least give the sport a try. In fact, by most standards, Kendall turned into a goal-scoring machine just one year later, at five – highlighted by one game where she scored eleven times. Intramural soccer made her a standout, if not a superstar, and then her first taste of travel soccer came as an eight-year-old. She did well enough to move three times in three years to better travel teams. Each time, she was driven to find better coaching and competition to challenge herself to improve.

But none were PDA. The level of play would be significantly higher than anything she had experienced to date. She had the innate talent, but she would have to make up ground on a group of kids that had already been competing at a higher level for three years.

Kendall had a passion for soccer, but she would need to turn that passion into drive to achieve this goal. It brought about what we expected to be a tough conversation.

"If you want to make PDA, you are going to need to work harder," we told her. This was a tall ask, because Kendall was already the type of kid that participated in extra training. As often as twice a week, give or take a session here and there.

"I know," she said. "How hard do I need to work?"

"Well, we don't really know," we told her. "But you have to stand out at a tryout that will likely feature hundreds of kids. And that's not easy. You should probably train every day."

This proclamation came at the end of December and tryouts were in May. In other words, we were suggesting that she train every day for over the next four months. Almost. The actual recommendation was to take off between three and five days in that time frame.

Yes, we feared burnout. But that lesson could wait. Instead, there was a different focus. Kendall had an audacious but attainable goal. So, we wanted to ensure she maximized the opportunity (and her talent) to reach her desired destination. She had to put everything on the table so there were no regrets. If she put in the effort, and didn't make it, Kendall could hold her head high no matter what.

"You are good enough," we told her. "But, if you want to play for that club you have to have passion and drive."

Passion to be (or play among) the best. Drive to practice until the requisite skills became second-nature.

Passion and drive.

Kendall understood and, with fun as the wind in her sails, she set out to harness that passion and drive to turn her aspiration into reality. Over the winter and early spring months, she rose to the occasion. She made sure to attend each of her team's trainings, also accepting invitations to train with other local teams. Kendall worked with local coaches in small group settings and signed up for private lessons as well.

During that same period of time, we were able to contact the head coach of one PDA team to see whether she could practice with the club and gauge how close she was to the club's level. She attended one practice and did well. Her passion and drive were paying off; but also reminded her of the task at hand. Kendall rose to the occasion, but she certainly realized how fast and dynamic the level of play was, admitting on the drive home that it overwhelmed her at first, and took her some time to adjust.

"See, your work is making you better," we said. "That commitment matters and if you stick with it, you'll make the team."

It was a great motivator. Kendall continued to dig in. There were adjustments, to be sure. She took maybe five days off when all was said and done, but she worked tirelessly keeping those three little letters in her sight.

By the end of April, with tryouts a few short weeks away, Kendall was simultaneously exhausted and exhilarated. She was playing her spring season at her current club and had already gone through their tryouts. But the excitement of an attainable goal, related to an activity she loved, kept her moving.

When the tryouts came and went, she had four months of passion and drive to push her forward at the very end. The preparation took over and she excelled. At the end of the second tryout, the coaches approached us to say they would be offering her a spot at the club.

It was amazing. It was exhausting. But passion and drive had gotten her to that point and it was most definitely time to celebrate.

Work hard, play hard
Anyone who has chased some type of goal has heard this mantra: work hard, play hard, and get great results. If you haven't heard that in your life, you probably just weren't listening.

But to what end? Too often hard work is a blanket concept that doesn't cultivate focus and efficiency. What does hard work typically mean? Do more. Work longer. Attack tasks with time. When you've put in that time, find more time to put in. Don't sleep. Give up balance. Give up everything else, if you really want to achieve the goal.

The problem with that approach is that it doesn't lead down any specific road.

If Kendall's had *just* worked hard to be a better soccer player, she may have accomplished the goal. But it's less likely that she would have known the best way to practice, or the skills on which to focus. As a nine-year-old girl, she didn't have the experience to design her own training sessions to maximize the requisite skills expected of a PDA athlete. How could she?

By working with the right trainers, and talking them through her very specific goals, she harnessed that hard work around a much-targeted purpose. She wanted to work *right*.

Kendall was driven to ensure she put the right time into the right things to maximize her personal development. That meant that her group training sessions were often with older kids, who were bigger and more physically developed. This emphasized development on her physicality – critical as a late bloomer who was smaller than most of her peers. It also meant she received feedback from private trainers, so she could further enhance her strengths and minimize her deficiencies. Drive kept her pushing to improve. Even when it wasn't comfortable.

Hard work versus drive

Let's dig in a little deeper, now that we've laid out the foundation for drive versus hard work.

Hard work and drive are often connected, or even used interchangeably. But that's wrong, because there's a difference. So, what is that difference? Let's start with the latter. Hard work is characterized by persistence. Most likely, there are long hours invested. Hard work is also characterized by consistent effort in order to deliver increased performance.

Drive takes hard work to the next level. When you're driven, there's no quantification of effort. You're not doing what's necessary to get the job done. Instead, the focus falls on excellence. Achievement. Or even greatness.

People that work hard count hours. People that are driven lose track of the hours as they chase a result. So, you do what's needed to be excellent, and that means the job is almost never done. As the quote goes in sports, "Don't practice until you get it right. Practice until you can't get it wrong."

Of course, in sports, there's always something else that requires such a level of commitment. Driven athletes, then, just keep going.

Those with drive continue when others stop. They work relentlessly to find a path toward the things that fuel, yes, their passion. Make sense?

It's important to note that drive can still burn you out. Those that are driven, in a vacuum, are driving toward the edge of a cliff. This pertains to individuals that have only short-term goals. Which brings us to the second key component of drive. If component one is putting in the work to achieve excellence, component two is applying that excellence to a long-term goal.

Why does a long-term goal matter? Because it sustains the drive. If you're simply driven for a short-term goal, it's easy to stop because there's no overarching desire to achieve new heights. It's the equivalent of pursuing a single sports skill instead of overall excellence. Here's an example. Imagine you dream of becoming an elite basketball player. Maybe, you see yourself in the mold of Steph Curry and mistakenly assume that becoming an expert three-point shooter is, alone, enough to achieve that goal. You're driven to become the best three-point shooter ever. This requires focus on mechanics, repetition and refinement.

Along the way, coaches tell you that Steph Curry is great for other reasons as well – he's an outstanding ball handler and passer. Neither are skills you really aspired to master, but they are certainly important to your pursuit of basketball excellence. If you're not driven, and you've already become a good three-point shooter, it's time to quit. The pursuit of excellence seems insurmountable. What you've done is work hard. You haven't demonstrated drive.

That all means that drive is constant and potentially never-ending. So, of course, it's possible that drive can exhaust you. It's possible that drive can burn you out.

Unless, that is, you have *passion* to keep you driven. Then it becomes passion and drive.

Fun versus passion

We talked about fun in the first chapter. Fun is a prerequisite to passion, but they are not the same. Fun is typically the foundation for passion. A building block, so to speak.

In other words, passion is the cumulative effect of the fun that one feels through small victories. As one achieves incrementally, fun builds. Passion then takes over. It becomes the fuel that sustains effort through times of tumult. It's the energy that pushes you through setbacks that occur when you pursue something with vigor.

Let's say that again: passion is what sustains the pursuit, specifically those pursuits that are fueled by drive. Here's how Merriam-Webster defines passion:

pas·sion
[pash-uh n]
noun
1. *any powerful or compelling emotion or feeling, as love or hate.*
2. *strong amorous feeling or desire; love; ardor.*

Fun is the drug, and passion is the addiction. Kendall started playing soccer more seriously because she had fun doing it. A moment is fun – making a great pass, scoring a goal, perfecting a skill. But it's the relentless pursuit of those fun moments that builds passion.

Training two, three, or four nights a week to develop the skills that will lead to consistent moments of fun – that's passion in action. Enjoying the effort required to position you for those fleeting moments, that requires passion.

Merriam-Webster may not embrace the drug-to-addiction continuum in its related analogies, but it's logical. Right?

So, Kendall had passion to sustain the drive, and that pushed her to

115 days of training in an effort to make PDA.

Passion and drive
Put it together then, and what do you have? Something incredibly special that can lead to success in life. Kendall had harnessed her passion, and added drive, to attain a goal. One that was unknowingly attainable. The key ingredients were passion and drive.

If you are passionate (insatiably thirsty or, yes, addicted) and driven (working toward an end without regard for the investment, but rather with an eye toward the outcome) it's arguable that you can achieve just about anything.

That's why, when youth sports bring those qualities out in your child, as they did with Kendall, the life lesson should be embraced, celebrated and savored. If you could take a picture of passion and drive, and frame it in a gaudy, ornate and obnoxious frame, you should. Hang it over the fireplace and show it off.

Since that's not really possible, tell your kid who is learning and living *passion and drive* just how proud you are of her at every turn.

Then figure out how to rediscover passion and drive in yourself and others, throughout other aspects of your life.

Dance, then dance some more
Hayden, our youngest, is the performer. She is obsessed with dance and other performance arts. Sure, she enjoys sports – and shoots a basketball pretty well. But her athletic prowess is nothing compared to her dance or music abilities.

Her participation and approach to these various activities illustrates the difference between passion and drive.

Let's go back to basketball as a starting point. She shoots well, considering how little time she spends practicing. And, considering her skills are unrefined, Hayden will *work hard* to get better when the opportunity presents itself. She may spend an hour in the driveway working on her footwork, release, and follow-through. After an hour, her jump shot will unquestionably improve. Hayden will go to basketball camp and work on other facets of her game as well, six hours a day for a week. She will most certainly enjoy every minute of it, and also get better along the way.

But, that's it. She won't go inside, then pick up a basketball and work on her ball-handling. She isn't driven the same way she is when dancing – as a contrast, she will come home and dance after her classes are over. When the prescribed basketball activities are done, she's finished with the pursuit. Hard work? Yes. Drive? Nope. Not this time.

Dance and piano, on the other hand, transcend hard work for her. Hayden possesses an insatiable passion for each of those crafts. That passion drives her to improve, with every possible moment at her disposal.

At the age of nine, she was taking twelve dance classes a week, with just two days off. Altogether, she was spending about eleven hours in a dance studio. And, yet, after dancing for three hours on a Thursday night, she would regularly come home and... dance... more ... a lot more. Two hours more, bringing her total for the day up to maybe five hours in a given situation. We would have to tell Hayden to stop dancing, so she could do homework or go to bed.

She didn't dance until she got something right; she danced until she couldn't get it wrong. If Hayden wanted to master a turn she had learned in class, she would work on it repeatedly. Passion and drive would show her the way.

I'm not improving on the piano

Earlier in the chapter, we explored how fun is foundational to leveraging passion and drive. In other words, when you've found the thing (or things) about which you care, make sure you're having fun so the passion and drive that push you into tough spots will also bring you out of them.

Learning how to play a musical instrument is tough. Really tough. Just like the development of any other skill, progress comes in fits and starts. Hayden had the same experience. For the first two years she played, progress was steady. Then, after switching teachers, she made a significant jump in her third and fourth years.

At Christmas time in her fourth year, she slammed into a wall at ninety miles per hour. The progress came to a screeching halt as she worked to learn a Christmas song for her holiday performance. She put the time in, but seemingly made the same mistakes over and over without really mastering the particular song.

The struggles frustrated her. She became irritated and sad. In this case, passion and drive started to work against her. With every practice session, she'd find herself stumbling at the same points. She continued to work hard at the same things, ending with the same results. When she messed up, she lost motivation.

Passion and drive brought her back to the piano over and over again. But the pursuit stopped being fun. She no longer enjoyed playing the piano due to repeatedly "failing" to progress past a certain point. She cried and wanted to quit.

Passion and drive were working against her because they kept her coming back and seemingly, kept pushing her to the point of failure.

It was time to combine life lessons. We took a step back and made sure that fun was the baseline again. It wasn't the piano that she disliked, it was this one particular song. Why even debate quitting when you love something? Just move on from the problem area, apply your passion and drive to another pursuit where you can find the fun – in this case another song. Once you've progressed, it's always possible to revisit the roadblock and defeat it. But don't let passion and drive work against you. Combine it with fun for the perfect formula of continued excellence.

Remember, we said that fun is the building block for passion, and that smaller successes build on each other, fueling that passion. In this case, one particular building block was cracking every time Hayden stepped on it. So, she needed to remove her foot from that block, and put it on another. Once she did, the climb resumed. She reminded herself of the fun foundation, and then passion and drive began moving in the right direction.

More than hard work, drive will take you places. Added to a passionate pursuit, you have the formula for amazing things. If soccer or any other youth sport can teach your child this life lesson, grab it and run with it.

Passion and Drive Actions
If you're fortunate enough to watch passion and drive motivate your child's pursuit of youth athletics, take note. Observe the behavior, praise it and reward it. Most likely, life once gave you a taste of passion and drive. Remind yourself of that time and recapture it, for yourself and others.

1. Learn your child's fun-to-passion spectrum. What makes things fun and where does that lead to passion? Where is it just fun for the sake of fun? Where you see the passion, build a series of goals.

2. Actively define "passion and drive" in the context of goals. Working hard doesn't mean working all the time. But it does

mean working with clarity, consistency and purpose. Know that excellence is the end goal, not time spent. Decide what the right level of drive is to achieve those goals.

3. Take a temperature check along the way. Find ways to gauge progress, then use them to reaffirm that passion and drive are being applied to the right things and are working.

4. Remind yourself that passions can change and when they do, it's ok. Specific drive can disappear if the passion dissipates. Passion and drive take significant effort, so be sure to put it in the right place.

5. Reward the behavior of passion and drive repeatedly. The outcomes don't matter because the behavior will lead to amazing things – you just may not know which application will be the ultimate one.

Chapter Three:
Make Mistakes

September 9th

Dear Diary,
Kendall is a few weeks into her fall soccer season, and I've noticed a recurring theme. She's playing well enough, but there's no fire. She's not as creative as she can be. Passing has always been her strength and it still is. But while she makes the simple pass, she's not making the breath-taking pass that draws the "oohs and ahhs" from parents on the sideline. It always used to be a staple of her game. No matter how she played or whether she scored, Kendall managed to pull an amazing pass out of her bag of tricks.

Now, it's nowhere to be found. Yes, Kendall is conservative by nature. But she never was on the soccer field. The field was where she could reinvent her personality and blend imagination with risk. And the results had been tremendous.

She's conservative on the field right now. I noticed it a few weeks ago. At first, she didn't want to talk about it. But lately, she has admitted that she's afraid to make mistakes. Her coach makes her feel like every mistake will be held against her. It will cost her playing time and ultimately relegate her to the bench.

Her coach doesn't encourage growth through error. What a shame. Athletes need to push their limits to maintain a growth mindset. For that matter, we all do. I want Kendall to make mistakes, so I need to find a way to encourage that. Wish me luck!

Sincerely,
Kent (aka, Soccer Dad)

Perfection is the enemy

It hurts to fail, so sometimes people don't even try. Which, frankly, is worse.

This was a constant challenge with Kendall as she first began to play soccer at a higher level. She is by her very nature, risk averse (admittedly, it's genetic). The root cause is perfectionism. Unless she's doing something perfectly, she feels like she's failing.

In its own right, that's not terrible. It does encourage hard work, which can be harnessed into drive with the right blend of passion. But it discourages a growth mindset. In the *Talent Code*, by Daniel Coyle, much credence was given to the idea that individuals with a growth mindset achieve more than people that adopt a fixed mindset.[4]

How the pursuit of perfection manifests itself is critical. For example, as Kendall became serious about soccer, she started participating in additional individual training activities – away from any team of which she was part.

This was a major commitment and one that demonstrated her seriousness for improvement. It was fun to watch because her natural technical talent was quite apparent. Kendall had an aptitude for techniques that required incredible coordination. Not only was she exceptional at the movements, but she could quickly pick up combinations and execute them with rapidity.

At first, she was free to experiment and fail, in large part because she excelled so rapidly compared to her peers in the same classes. That buffer meant she would fall more into a growth mindset than she might otherwise – making mistakes and still being the best relative

---

[4] Coyle, Daniel. *The Talent Code: Greatness Isn't Born. It's Grown. Here's How.* (New York: Bantam, 2009)

to everyone else in her class made it easier to let perfectionism slide. She progressed very quickly within her training age group, moving into an older age group twice by the time she was nine.

That's when the risk aversion became a problem. As Kendall trained with older kids, she continued to focus on refinement and mastery of the movements, techniques and combinations. However, to apply that technical ability successfully against bigger, stronger and more experienced competition, she had to take risks. No longer could she make mistakes and separate herself from other players in her training sessions. She needed to take *bigger* touches (meaning, when she would manipulate a soccer ball she would have to push the ball further away from her, for example, and still keep control), make *faster* cuts, or demonstrate *creativity* unlike anything she had done before.

And she needed to do those things to the point where she was almost making mistakes every time she attempted a skill. To take that next step in her development, she needed to push beyond safe and challenge herself to find that next avenue of growth.

Making those mistakes would be the best thing that happened to her. Operating on the edge of her comfort zone, Kendall would find a new level of ability. The only problem, of course, was that perfectionism prevented it. She would train more conservatively, not less. The growth mindset was stymied by fear of making mistakes that would be magnified by better and older competition.

Getting over it
Everyone is different, but very few people truly and inherently embrace making mistakes. Kendall is no exception. She was such a perfectionist that mistakes definitely upset her. She hated them. That equated to continued conservatism. Kendall wouldn't push herself in the ways described above. Consequently, she obtained mixed results as she trained against better competition. To her,

mixed results, didn't feel like growth. They felt like failure.

She refused to fail. But in her steadfast refusal, she wasn't really succeeding either.

Trainers would tell her...

> *Kendall, make that touch bigger!*
> *Kendall, you can do it faster!*
> *You need to push yourself to the point of making mistakes if you want to get better.*
> *Train as hard as you can.*
> *This is the place to make mistakes so you're ready for the games!*

She heard them, but she couldn't immediately make the adjustment. It was simply contrary to her personality.

As a parent, the immediate reaction is to want your child to achieve objectives that you know are within their grasp. Objectives they want to reach. *Kendall, just believe in yourself, you can do it!* Encouraging her to forget her perfectionism in the name of soccer excellence... well, that's the path to a college scholarship. See, it's just that easy to fall back into the youth sports trap.

A moment of reflection, however, brings about a key life lesson. Kendall has the talent. Kendall's aversion to making mistakes was clearest when pushed past comfort. For her, that felt like failure, not the place where the greatest growth took place. Not the route to get even better than she already was as a soccer player. Trainers saw how easily she could master techniques and knew that her improvement would come at times of great discomfort.

She simply couldn't get her head around that idea. To her, mistakes were just mistakes, not opportunities to grow. She had to make an adjustment. This would truly be moving forward. Whether challenging herself in math, science, writing, knitting, art, robotics… anything! The life lessons observed while hiding on the sidelines was clear – we needed to encourage Kendall to make mistakes. Not just to make them, but also seek them. Or, eventually, embrace them.

We set about methodically talking through the concepts of fixed versus growth mindsets. Soccer was the perfect playground for this life lesson.

Now versus later
For Kendall, that meant taking a step back and reminding her that training was not, in itself, the end goal. She trained to improve her soccer skills. She improved her soccer skills, so she would have mastery of them when it was time to put on a uniform and play games.

Let's say that again, you train to develop skills you can use in the game.

In practice, that idea can produce the opposite of a growth mindset. Why? Because when you draw a line that must be crossed, you act differently on both sides of that line. Sure, you train to excel. For example, Kendall was free to make mistakes in practices where she was clearly the best athlete, but when she trained with older kids, she was less prone to make "mistakes". If you set the belief that it's ok to take risks in practice, but not in games, you'll draw the same arbitrary line.

The reality is that none of it truly matters unless you want it to. If your child decides that sports matter, then make sure they know that mistakes help them grow regardless of the outcome. It's a continuum of growth that starts the moment you begin playing and ends only when you hang up your cleats. If you focus on the lessons in this book, it doesn't really end when you hang them up, either.

With Kendall, we had to continually emphasize this concept. The time to push herself and make mistakes was not just in training, but also during games. And making mistakes was actually the way to get better.

How can your child adopt this same mindset? Testing herself. Her strengths. Her limits. Pushing too far past them and failing. Understanding why. Correcting it. During practices, during games and everywhere in between.

The science behind skills acquisition and programming within the body is meticulously outlined. This is yet another concept well documented by Coyle in the *Talent Code*. The more you do something, the more your body builds matter around the neurons that fire during a specific skill.[5] So repetition matters. The way you create those repetitions also matters. Making mistakes then refining your specific movements by learning from those mistakes is a concept dubbed *deep practice*. The more you partake in *deep practice*, the more refined the skill.

Mistakes aren't part of that process. They are, in fact, the primary catalyst for the entire process. For people that are mistake-averse and perfection-driven, this feels counterintuitive and can be downright painful. But, the value of mistakes has to be stated and repeated, and then applied.

The more we dug into the purpose of training and the role of mistakes, the more Kendall understood that her long-term excellence depended on making and correcting them.

Slowly, she became more comfortable pushing herself in training and practice because she realized the long-term objective. That was

---

[5] Coyle, Daniel. *The Talent Code: Greatness Isn't Born. It's Grown. Here's How.* (New York: Bantam, 2009)

the key takeaway. We had to remind her of the objectives, explain their role in training, and show how pushing herself to the point of making mistakes facilitated that process.

The process started with small steps. In a training session, we would suggest focusing on one skill. Not to perfect, but to break. When she challenged herself to the point of making errors, there was constant and positive reinforcement. Were we proud of her excellence during fifty-five minutes of training? Sure. But we were far prouder of the five minutes she pushed herself to a level of discomfort.

From there, it expanded. In the next training sessions, we suggested a longer period of discomfort, like ten minutes, or stretching herself on two skills. As she progressed, we extended the recommendations during each training event.

Eventually, something interesting happened. Kendall completely changed her approach to training. We would watch her for sixty minutes and conclude that she had struggled or simply didn't have it. But when she came off the field and began talking about her session, she was thrilled with her performance. Why? Because she had spent those sixty minutes making mistakes. It may not have looked clean or excellent to the naked eye, but she had, for the entire hour, been practicing with a purpose. She knew where she was weak and focused on improving that weakness.

Kendall didn't immediately take the same approach into her games. That took longer. Much longer. But it did happen, and, within a few years, she was actively taking risks and making mistakes in games that "mattered." She knew that any particular game was a small point on a continuum. Any game was far more important if it extended the continuum than if that game became an end to itself.

Kendall learned how to make mistakes, one small step at a time.

It's always a process

This lesson evolved as this book was being written. Make no mistake, when you're an inherent perfectionist, there's no escaping that mindset. You constantly have to work on adjusting to appreciate and embrace growth versus fixed mentalities. It's a life-lesson, to be sure. These behaviors take constant recalibration.

Just as your child figures out how to manage negative emotional reactions to one process, another problem will arise, and she has to figure out how to deal with it as well.

Most people never become naturally good at dealing with mistakes. But it's a practice. One that will make your child better. The more open someone is to recognizing and managing those scenarios, the more she will constantly improve.

When your child is inevitably overcome by perfectionism, take a step back and remind her that mistakes will help her grow. And that growth will make her better than she is right now. Then ask her this simple question: Would you rather be a perfect version of your current self, or better than you can possibly imagine right now by making mistakes along the way?

It's just a test

There may be no better "non-sports" application of this principle than in the classroom. Children spend more time there than anywhere else, except maybe in their bed.

In many ways, increasing classroom pressures mirror those associated with youth sports. School is not a place where kids feels safe to make mistakes and learn. Premiums are put on performance and outcomes. Additional value is put on attendance and compliance. Its rigidity is the formula by which a school's value is measured.

Earn good grades to make the honor roll. Earn good grades to achieve a high-class rank. Earn good grades so you can get into college. Achieve high test scores to get into honors classes. Achieve high test scores to get into college. Do all of that so you can get a job. Most likely a desk job, that is intended to reduce risk.

Student experiences aren't driven by the desire to acquire and apply critical thinking skills as much as they are laden with the lofty parental and teacher expectations related to outcomes. This is the reason so many tests are met with student anxiety. Kids don't see them as opportunities to apply and refine skills they've acquired. Instead, they see the pressure of expectations.

Recall that Kendall is a perfectionist by nature – in school and on the soccer field. So, she takes great pride in working hard to achieve outcomes in those areas. It leads to strong grades and test scores.

It was validation, then, that encouraging mistakes – not being afraid to make them and also accepting that they will happen and that you can learn from them – had carried over from the soccer field to the school room on its own. This was demonstrated most clearly when annual standardized testing brought about a big mistake.

Kendall came home from school one day to explain that she had completely missed a free-response question while completing a standardized test. She knew the consequences – there was no chance for a perfect score and she most likely would lose a few percentage points based on that mistake alone!

The instructions were confusing, and I just skipped over it.

She continued by telling us that she didn't realize the error until the allotted time was consumed. She noticed the mistake later, when completing a different section of the test.

Kendall relayed that, if dishonest, she could have completed the missed question during the next testing period, which was focused on a different topic. They kept that first answer sheet, and she had time left to go back and finish it. No one would have ever known. But, she said, that wasn't the right thing to do.

I made a mistake, but that's ok. I'll just learn from it and improve next time.

Those were her words. Not ours. She recognized that taking a short-cut would have, in essence, overshadowed the lesson. In fact, it would have taught her a different and negative lesson. What were the positive lessons? There were a few. Be more thorough. Re-read instructions. Double-check that everything assigned has been completed.

These were lessons she needed to learn. Kendall's intelligence allowed her to often overlook details but allowed her to achieve success without consequences. Only by making a mistake, with real consequences, would she reflect and make a change.

That sounds a lot like her experience with soccer training, right? Her aptitude allowed her to excel against kids her age – she could make small mistakes and still be the best. But only when she competed against older kids, when her mistakes were maximized with greater consequences, did she learn lessons that caused her to reflect and make changes.

Her experience on the field had prepared her for inevitable mistakes. When a mistake occurred in the classroom, she was prepared to assess, understand and accept its impacts. As a result, she understood the value of the mistake itself and knew that there are many things in life that are far more important than a standardized test score.

It's hard to accept mistakes. Sports provide a unique opportunity to encourage them. You can explore the upsides and downsides of how they are handled and apply those experiences to almost anything else you do.

Make Mistakes Actions

How can you focus on cultivating a growth mindset? All of the behaviors explored in this book have challenges and this is among the most challenging of the group. While we provide actions for exploring each life lesson and influencing behaviors to empower young athletes and parents alike, the freedom to make mistakes requires constant action. Here are some that will help.

1. This is going to seem simple, but talk about the value of making mistakes. Sometimes perfectionists – those that hate mistakes the most – are among the most analytical people around. Working through the logic of error and the value of a growth mindset will give them the resources needed to adopt it.

2. Fear is typically the emotion blocking failure. Find and explore examples of failure that have resulted in dramatic growth. Two sports examples immediately come to mind – basketball legend Michael Jordan being cut from his high school basketball team and all-time great quarterback Tom Brady falling to pick 199 in the NFL draft. If "failure" can drive two sports legends, it can help you.

3. Modeling behavior is critical. Share your own vulnerabilities as a parent with your child. Then show them how you will push yourself to make mistakes in your own life and grow from them.

4. Focus on one area of growth, not many. While it's great to make mistakes, going from perfectionist to a person who wants to fix "everything" is impossible. Focusing on an area

of particular apprehension – just one – and overcoming the fixed mindset will unlock doors. Stay focused.

5. Recalibrate after you've mastered something that was once a stretch. Just because a specific growth opportunity becomes an area of mastery doesn't mean the behavior should end. Find the next place where mistakes will become the tools for growth and focus energy there.

Chapter Four:
Chauffeur

September 14th

Dear Diary,
My soccer career ended when I was twelve or thirteen (I can't even remember specifically) so I could focus all of my energy on baseball. Most parents want to help their kids as they grow in a sport. But, it became pretty clear to me a few years ago that I could support and encourage Kendall's growth, but I certainly couldn't help coach soccer-specific skills. She was better than I had ever been by the time she was ten.

For the last few days, that was bothering me. I felt like I couldn't offer much that would help her development. But then it occurred to me, that's not true. There are a few key things I will always need to do as my daughter pursues soccer. The first is to be her biggest fan.

The second job I have is to be her chauffeur. Yep, that's right, I have to drive her everywhere she needs to be when playing soccer. Driving her to and from the field is critical. I help set the direction, get her pointed the right way and then ensure she gets to go out and pursue her goals.

Plus, we get to talk a lot, which is pretty great. Chauffeur literally, and figuratively? Shouldn't all parents embrace this role to help their kids? I want to explore the importance of that with Kendall.

Sincerely,
Kent (aka, Soccer Dad)

Looking inward

So far, we've talked about how to help your child prepare before they get to the field. Emphasizing fun, passion and drive, and making mistakes gets them in the right mindset to play. But, this chapter is a bit different. Here, we focus on a parental behavior that can have a major impact on the values your child learns from his participation in sports. Actually helping your child get to the field so he can play.

It may seem like a thankless job in some ways. But, really, there is ample opportunity to talk about the sport, and all life lessons associated with it, while travelling to and from the field. Commuting with your child can be done several different ways – walking, driving and beyond. Our experience is connected to car rides, so we'll focus on that for the purpose of this chapter. But, you can certainly apply the lessons explored here in any such setting. You just have to do it right. That's where focusing on parental behaviors, and their impact on a young athlete's behavior, takes center stage. In the car, how you act has a direct impact on how your child acts. And you spend lots of time in the car, together, as a result of participation in youth sports. That means you have to be a chauffeur. More importantly, you have to be a *good chauffeur*.

Visit any youth sporting event – soccer game, baseball game, football game, or even a *practice*. Very quickly, you'll see a common and disturbing theme. Parents believe they are secondary coaches.

Regardless of how qualified your child's actual coach is, some parents on your team will think they can better instruct a group of ten-year-old kids to excel. Often, this extends from parents yelling at their own kids to feeling it's appropriate (or valuable, bafflingly) *to coach other people's kids.*

This behavior seemingly starts from a good place. Parents genuinely want to help their child "succeed" in terms of performance. But it rapidly transforms into the manifestation of early achievement envy.

Parents want their kid to be the best, or to keep up with the best. They begin urging them to execute on a level that will make them stand out. Why? It's probably different for everyone. Some parents think they can provide that edge to catapult their daughter from the second team to the first team, or from first team substitute player to starter, or from starter to star.

Others are focused on college scholarships before their son has even hit puberty. And a third segment genuinely *knows* (they go far past belief, far too quickly) their daughter will play on the United States Women's National Team and become a household name.

Their coaching, of course, will be the difference.

NOTE: If you are reading this and can't think of anyone whose behavior pushes this extreme, it's probably you. Keep reading.

The coach knows more than you
The reality is that, regardless of the level at which your child is playing, the person wearing the coaching hat can do a better job than you. Even if he's not an experienced coach. If someone has dedicated his time to coaching, he is putting effort into preparation. He's getting to know the kids and working to make them as a unit. When all of those things are true, your individualized sideline coaching is often less thoughtful and potentially contrary to the coach's messages.

There are exceptions. When you deal with parent coaches that destroy fun or distort perspective because of nepotism, some sideline coaching may be warranted. But, for the most part, it has a negative impact on the team and your child.

Imagine, just for a moment, how your child feels standing on the field trying to work as one with a group of girls she spends twelve hours with each week, as you scream at each and every one of them to do more or do better. These are her friends that you're offending. For what? Let the coach handle that.

In situations where your child participates at a high-level, with paid coaches who have gone through various licensing processes, there's no question the coach knows more than you. That's just reality. They've reached that point through hard work, or maybe passion and drive, mixed with a deeper understanding of their sport. You may not agree with their philosophies, but they are valid.

That was the hard realization that came with Kendall's progression. Parental coaching was no longer necessary, helpful (if it ever was) or warranted. She was being coached by professionals. Individuals that played at the highest levels – elite college programs and sometimes even professionally – and who had earned their stripes. They were students of the craft, working on it every day.

Her coaches simply knew more. So, coaching from the sidelines is fruitless and often counterproductive.

It doesn't end there. Your child knows more than you also. Just as Kendall did by the age of nine. She trained three, four or five times a week. Playing at an elite club meant she had mastered key skills and concepts of soccer faster than most people ever master skills in any chosen discipline.

You have to find another way and another place to be a positive influence on your child and enrich the experience. Can't think of one? Let us help.

What's the job then?
When that realization finally hits a soccer parent, and there's enough self-control to change sideline behavior, what's left?

It's a fair question. How do you go from a *coaching* mentality to something else? Of course, you're a fan, which also takes on a very specific functional role. But, we'll talk more about that later.

In this case, how do you replace to urge (the need) to feel like you're contributing to the development of your son or daughter's athletic skills? For a younger child, it's still vital that you participate in their activities. The most critical resources you can provide to your kids are time and attention. So there has to be a way to focus those particular resources productively.

Take a step back and think about the mechanics of being a soccer parent and the answer becomes clear. You're not the one putting on practice clothes and stepping onto the field to kick a soccer ball. You're not the one building camaraderie with teammates and working towards a common goal. You're not the one playing in pressure-packed games.

Instead, you are keeping them moving towards those goals. You are helping ensure the practice clothes are clean. That they are getting dressed and filling their water jugs early enough to arrive on time. Then, the majority of your time is spent driving them to and from practice. That's the critical role in which you've been cast for your child's athletic play.

You're the driver. Your job is chauffeur. That's right, driving your kids to and from soccer practice or games is potentially the most important job you have in their journey.

Does it seem unfulfilling when that realization finally hits you? Oh well, that's reality. So, you might as well deal with it. Actually, let's do better. You might as well maximize it. Be great at it, the same way you probably want your child to be great at soccer or some other sport.

Yes, that's right, become a great chauffeur.

It's more important than you think

Being the driver doesn't seem terribly glamorous. It may not even seem that important. But it truly is. Think about the impact your commitment to driving has on your children's development.

1. You get them to a required destination.
2. You get them there on a schedule.
3. You demonstrate support by giving your time.
4. You give them a period of time (whether it's five minutes or forty-five minutes) to talk and connect.
5. You very literally show them the way.
6. You demonstrate respect for rules (arrival times, traffic rules, etc.).
7. You solve problems (get gas, change routes, deal with traffic).
8. You lead through example.

In other words, you're giving them structure and resources required to pursue something important, with associated short and long-term goals. Short term – prepare to get out the door and then get to practice on time. Long term – make practice a priority so you can improve, perform well and continue playing the sport you love.

You're still part of the process, just a different part of the process.

What you don't do is try to play the game for your child. Drivers don't sit in the passenger seat at the same time they drive. That's the equivalent of parents trying to coach. Instead, drive them and then wait for them to come back to the car like any good chauffeur does. Of course, unlike a real chauffeur, you don't have to stay in the car and out of sight. You can and should, at times, watch your child play. Just in a way that's inconspicuous.

Being a chauffeur offers ample drive time and opportunity to participate in other ways. We'll talk about that in the next chapter.

But, for now, focus on driving.

How it plays out
Without getting into the "front seat driver" context, let's explore how interacting with your child on the way to the field goes and how you can impact your child's behavior by deploying the best chauffeur behaviors of your own.

Good chauffeuring starts before you even get in the car. Consider professional drivers. If you hire one to drive to the airport, their job doesn't start when they get to your house. It starts well before that. They have to map out the route from origin to your house to final destination. They have to ensure the car is clean, has a full tank of gas, and stocked with water. They have to get dressed. They have to leave on time to arrive on time.

The same is true for your chauffeur job, but you're typically taking similar steps in conjunction with your child.

> *Kendall, it's time to get ready to leave.*

Invariably, there's pushback.

> *I am getting ready.*
> *Why haven't you started to get dressed then?*
> *Well, it only takes me five minutes.*
> *True, but you still need to get your clothes out of the laundry, pack your bag and make sure you have cleats.*
> *Ok, I know.*
> *Great. I'm glad you know. But let me just remind you that we have to get out the door in about ten minutes and those things will take that long. So, unless you want to be late for practice, you should hustle. Plus, practice is early tonight so we might hit some traffic.*

This seems like such a banal exchange, but it's critically important.

You're setting a driving strategy for your daughter, and then outlining the tactics that get you there. At the age of ten or even twelve, these steps are likely not yet obvious to her.

As a chauffeur, you've done so much to help your daughter pursue her soccer ambitions, and you're not even in the car yet.

Then, once you get into the car, it continues.

> *Hey, did you make sure to pack a snack?*
> *Yes, dad (eye rolls ensue).*
> *Great. Did you eat your whole lunch at school today?*
> *Yes, dad (more eye rolls).*
> *Are you sure?*
> *Well, I didn't eat my whole sandwich.*
> *Ok, why don't you drink some water and eat that granola bar. Maybe even a few strawberries. It's hot outside and you'll need to stay hydrated and you'll need the energy.*

You haven't even begun to navigate the drive – and frankly, that's pretty obvious, so we won't outline that. Yet, you've delivered incredible value to your daughter in the capacity of chauffeur. Embrace it and be great at it. With every drive you take, modeling behaviors that translate strategy into tactics. Short-term direction into long-term pursuits.

Be a great chauffeur.

I want to dance
There will be a moment when it's over. When your child no longer wants to play the sport at all. That's why this book exists – know it's ok and that as long as you maximize critical life lessons associated with the sport, it will have been worthwhile regardless of how long it lasted.

It may end when they're adults and your direct parental influence feels like it has long since diminished. More likely, your daughter's soccer days will end sometime between the ages of nine and, say, twenty.

If you are statistically normal, in the seventy percent of athletes that quit by the age of thirteen and never play sports again, then you may one day face this random dinner conversation in the middle of the winter.[6]

I don't want to play soccer anymore. It's not fun and I spend too much time doing it.

As caring parents, you eventually come to understand this decision. It may take a while. After all, you've put years of energy into supporting the pursuit of a sport, and then it just ends in a flash. For you. Understand that your child has been building to that moment for quite some time. Maybe there are tears. But once they subside, logic ultimately rules out.

When this happens, basic parenting takes over. You want to ensure your daughter is spending all of the newly found free time in the most productive manner – not just transferring her soccer time to socializing or texting.

Don't worry, she's already ahead of you.

I've always wanted to dance again. Can I sign up for ballet this fall?

Your head races. Immediately, you begin fighting the achievement and outcome mindset. Yes, she took two years of ballet when she

---

[6] Julianna W. Miner, "Why 70 percent of kids quit sports by age 13," *The Washington Post*, June 1, 2016,
https://www.washingtonpost.com/news/parenting/wp/2016/06/01/why-70-percent-of-kids-quit-sports-by-age-13.

was four and five years old. But, now, at thirteen, it's highly unlikely your daughter will excel enough as a ballerina to warrant a college scholarship... or professional consideration... or...

STOP.

Maybe ballet will be fun. Maybe she will find passion in its pursuit. Maybe she will be driven to learn new skills rapidly. Maybe she we will be comfortable making mistakes. Ballet may provide an amazing platform to continue learning the life lessons we've discussed so far.

(And, you never actually know how discovering a passion late can turn out. Famous ballerina Misty Copeland didn't start dancing until she was nearly thirteen.)[7]

Regardless, one thing is very, very clear. Your daughter has picked a new destination. It may not be her ultimate destination – maybe just a stop along the way. But, your job is to help her map the coordinates, figure out a route and drive her. You're the chauffeur. That's the job. Just as it was before. The destination has changed, but the job stays the same. Give her a comfortable seat, make sure to talk to her along the way.

You are no longer ensuring she is dressed for soccer, but instead for dance. You are probably driving her to a studio and not a field. But you're still a chauffeur, and she has teachers (not coaches). That's not only ok, but it's also important.

I don't want to go to that private school
You may face the same challenge with school choices. It's always been your dream to have your son go to private school.

---

[7] Aaron Hicklin, "Misty Copeland: dancing into history," *The Guardian*, March 5, 2017, https://www.theguardian.com/stage/2017/mar/05/misty-copeland-principal-american-ballet-theatre-life-in-motion.

Yes, as a good chauffeur, you not only drive but sometimes also suggest destinations of interest to your passengers. Thinking that matriculation into a top private school may be a good option for your child certainly falls into that category. Maybe you urge him to take entrance exams. Then he applies and does well enough to hit the interview phase.

A prestigious school not only accepts your son, but also offers him a scholarship. Tuition was the only real concern – but they removed that roadblock with a scholarship. So, the path is clear!

But, then your son takes the next step. A visitation day. He will have the opportunity to spend time with the current students, and experience life as he would when enrolled.

He hates it. A day at the school makes him appreciate how much he enjoys his current public-school setting. How much he likes exposure to a large student body and the opportunities that come with it.

His course has changed. His destination has changed. As his chauffeur, that means your plans change as well. You hit exit on the current set of directions in the GPS – based on the one your passenger suggests this time – and enter a new stop. Hit the brakes, turn right and start down the next path.

If that's your approach, you've done your job as a chauffeur. Suggest a course, drive it, then when the passenger decides it's not for him, change it and start down another. Provide guidance along the way, listen and keep moving forward.

I don't want to go to that college
Repeat the script above the college selection process. If your son would prefer to attend Penn State as opposed to the University of Pennsylvania (no, they aren't the same school…Go Quakers), be

appreciative that he saved you hundreds of thousands of dollars. Be confident that he'll figure out how to best maximize his destination, then put your chauffeur hat on and drive him there.

Or, look at the example in reverse. If you are concerned about your son's financial well-being and encourage him to attend Penn State to avoid school loans and long-term debt, but he has his heart set on Penn, drive him there. Of course, advise him of the difference in financial commitment and the long-term implications. Advise him vigorously. But, still, drive him to Penn.

That's your job.

I don't want that career
Ok, so you were fine with the college choice after some heartburn and tears.

But, your dream (see all of the parental dreams emerging all of a sudden?) has always been for him to become a doctor. And, it's definitely going to happen. His aptitude for math and science is outstanding. High school grades that could have gotten him into Ivy League schools remained elite during his time at Penn State (in the honors program no less). He aced the MCATs. This dream most certainly maps to reality.

Except, that outstanding Science Technology Engineering and Math (STEM) brain he possesses was being put to a different use in between class. Little did you know he was becoming an exceptional computer engineer. And starting a business – he developed an app that hadn't made much money but became popular enough to warrant the interest of the industry's best tech companies.

Medical school wasn't an option. He was planning to become a software engineer and eventually a tech founder.

Again, put on your chauffeur hat and drive. Help him get to the chosen destination. The reality is, if you don't, he will. Driving himself might take longer, and you won't be involved. So, accept the job and embrace it.

Understanding this role is critical for a parent and incredibly comforting for a child. You get the opportunity to put it into very literal practice through soccer and other youth sports. Focus on how to maximize it and the lesson will translate well to other areas of life.

Chauffeur Actions
How can you become a great chauffeur? The behaviors related to this life lesson are tough for some to practice because they require patience. For "Type A" personalities, keeping your eyes on the road and hands on the wheel, while passengers plot the tactical future, can be a unique challenge. But, embracing this role can be among the most rewarding in a sports parent's life.

1. Make sure you really know the destination. This sounds silly, but it takes preparation. Too often soccer parents don't double check the location of a game or practice. It shows preparation and commitment. You can only be a great chauffeur if you know where you're actually taking your passenger.

2. Get comfortable with silence. Once you buy into the notion that driving your passenger to the designated destination requires parallel performance – you getting there and her getting ready for what happens once you get there – you realize that silence is productive.

3. Prepare for empathy. Know where your passenger is going and consider the potential outcomes at the destination to which you've driven. What could go wrong and how can you demonstrate an emotional connection to the situation.

If you're not prepared, you are likely to have your own reaction instead of relating to hers.

4. Similarly, know what outcomes you should reward. Your passengers will be focused on outcomes, which is awesome. But when things go right, you have a fantastic opportunity as the chauffeur to reinforce the life lessons we're exploring in this book. When your passenger scores a goal, consider the rewards and recognition should be focused on the passion and drive that got them to this point.

5. Practice over-communicating when you're not driving. The only way to give plenty of information at the right time is to become the type of person that gives it all of the time. Chauffeurs over communicate when they're not in the car, so it's easier to stay silent when they are in the car.

Chapter Five:
Front-Seat Coaching

September 17th

Dear Diary,
I've decided that the chauffeur thing is really important. I got that part right.

But, it's not easy! Sure, driving your child around seems simple enough. Remember how I said it's great that we get time to talk? That's not necessarily true. Well, let me clarify that. It is great that we have time to talk. But, you have to be really careful what you talk about.

Specifically, it's better not to talk about soccer. Seems crazy, right? I mean, we're on our way to and from soccer. And if we want to talk about what Kendall's actually doing then that would be the logical topic.

Except, it never seems to go well. This one is tough.

There's no easy answer. I've decided to work at it and find a really productive way to use that time. There are good reasons not to discuss soccer. I definitely don't want that time to be negative when it can be so positive.

I'll let you know how it goes.

Sincerely,
Kent (aka, Soccer Dad)

Beyond driving

In the previous chapter, we talked about driving. About being a chauffeur. We didn't adequately talk about how to handle the piece of being a driver that has nothing to do with driving – interacting with your passengers.

Some drives are long. Over the course of a week, you may spend six hours (or more) in the car with your child driving to and from sporting events. You may want to give them time to recharge before talking to your child, but that can only last so long. At some point, conversation will creep into the mix. If you're really playing the role of a chauffeur correctly, using that conversation time requires adherence to another life lesson: be a great front-seat coach.

What exactly does that mean?

Participating in youth sports is increasingly high stakes, which means it is also quite emotional and exhausting. The drive to and from practices or games are opportunities for young athletes to mentally prepare for a game, or unwind one from one, respectively. Its critical to refrain from commentary during the drive to and from the activities. That's good front-seat coaching.

Make no mistake, you can be a terrible one. Bad front-seat coaching is when you do just the opposite. On the way to a game, you are providing a complete game plan with specific instructions. Your suggestions aren't suggestions at all. They are directives. You put the pressure on your child before she steps foot on the field.

On the way home, the bad front-seat coach is even worse. It's not even that they want to break down the game. That can be ok, though it's definitely not ideal. Instead, as soon as their child's butt hits the seat after getting in the car, they begin breaking down everything that could and should have been done better.

Why didn't you run harder?
Why did you miss that pass?
Why didn't you score?

And this is, often, after an excellently played game. It can be devastating to your child. These interactions can, in fact, be the primary reason the sport is no longer fun. The primary reason they stop playing.

The key lesson here is to avoid bad front-seat coaching. Focusing on the outcomes, desired or actual, does more damage than good. Use targeted drive and talk time to emphasize the value youth sports has to your child's life.

Leveraging a business approach
Parents can apply work behaviors to this lesson. Many soccer parents work in corporate America and have spent time contemplating the qualities of their managers and leaders. They can attest to the idea that a chauffeur must definitely be a manager. He must manage the tactics of the trip to and from the field.

Great parent chauffeurs, like great managers, also have leadership qualities. They help provide that critical vision. Then they make their team, or children, believe they can achieve their goals. The continually propel them forward as a good front-seat coach.

Your time in the car, when aiming to be the best possible front-seat coach, is also the time to flex leadership muscles. Taking this comparison a bit further, we can leverage instruction from the business world to inform how parents or coaches should act in leadership scenarios and become that great front-seat coach.

An Inc. magazine article outlines six key things great leaders "give" their team. Each principle can be applied to how you interact with a passenger.[8] Replace the word "employee" with child, and you have a model of leadership in a front-seat coaching scenario. We've done so in parentheses.

Give (your child) your ear. The great cliché is passengers spilling their deepest, darkest secrets to cab drivers. Why does the relationship go this way? Likely for practical reasons. The driver is focused on the destination, and the passenger is thinking about the tasks required to get there, or to prepare for being there. When you drive, the destination (strategy and long-term goals) is your focus. When you're in the passenger seat, you have the journey (what turn is required, what thinking can be done during the trip) more in mind. For soccer players and parents, the parallels are clear. Parents are just trying to make sure they don't miss a turn that will make them late. Children are getting on their socks and shin guards, wondering if they'll start and focusing on how they'll play that day. Good front-seat coaches, then, can be a fantastic sounding board for their children as they work through the emotional rollercoaster of a situation.

Give (your child) your empathy. Soccer kids are too young to drive. In a figurative sense, they aren't ready to drive anyway. They are still learning the roads, making mistakes and growing as a human. When bad times are upon them, they know when they've screwed up. The last thing they need is a lecture during a proverbial ride. What children do need is empathy – they want to know that you understand how hard it was for them to miss the game-winning shot, or perform poorly on a test, or make a mistake of naivete. The most important time to signal empathy is when they come

---

[8] Marcel Schwantes, "To Be a Strong Leader, There Are 6 Things You Must Give Your People (Most Rarely Do)," *Inc.*, May 25, 2017, https://www.inc.com/marcel-schwantes/to-be-a-strong-leader-there-are-6-things-you-must-give-your-people-most-rarely-d.html.

off the field and you're driving home. The immediate response sets the tone.

Give (your child) rewards and recognition. Sports and life are emotional. When someone sets a goal and then implements a plan of passion and drive to reach it, they expend immense energy. Personality types dictate their motivation – whether they are internally or externally motivated plays a factor in just how they get there. Either way, rewards and recognition for their efforts make your child feel seen, understood and appreciated. Again, the car ride – the immediate period of time following the achievement – is the time to get this right. For the very same reasons you demonstrated empathy instead of criticism after a mistake, you need to heap rewards and recognition quickly. If you are taking your role as front-seat coach seriously, it's really the most important thing you have to do at the time.

Give (your child) space to recharge. Imagine that your son has either screwed up or absolutely crushed their goals. Either extreme works here. And you played the first part of the role perfectly – demonstrating empathy or rewarding and recognizing them at the peak of emotional saturation. Step two is just as important. You have a forty-five-minute car ride home from a game. The natural inclination is to debrief. How did you screw up and why? How did you succeed and why? These are learning lessons after all and it's critical to embrace them. That's totally true, but not right away. Once you've completed step one, step two is NOT to dig deep into the outcomes of a particular action. Step two is to back off and let your child recharge. Most likely, they have spent weeks, months or even years preparing for a given outcome. The lessons learned don't have to be addressed in the immediate aftermath and any attempt to do so will feel like emotional noise. Great front-seat coaches don't talk their way through long drives, they let their passengers' recharge.

Give their (child) plenty of information, communicating both good and bad. When you set the direction and take charge of getting your passenger to a particular location, sometimes the world takes you on a detour. In those cases, a ten-minute trip may turn into a thirty-minute trip. Your passenger needs to know what's going on. Providing information on strategic and tactical changes and communicating information that will impact him is critical. For your athletic child, this means ensuring he knows as fast as possible that a late arrival to practice is in the works and there's nothing that can be done to fix it. For your student child, it means talking through how test results or grade will impact his various options – taking advanced classes the following year or which college may accept them. Too often parents withhold information because they believe it will "protect" the feelings of their child or control potential anxieties. Keeping your passenger in the dark just takes him out of the "zone" required to perform. It's far easier for him to adjust if he understands that detours will be required.

Give the (child) fairness. At first, connecting fairness to the front-seat coaching job may not seem obvious. In reality, being a great front-seat coach means being fair, and trading on actions instead of emotions. If you set the route and then decide to drive, you have to give your child a ride no matter what their chosen destination. When you are driving to and from the same place, you can apply each of the concepts to any passenger. Good leaders and parents will do just that.

These behaviors aren't easy for a sports parent and they certainly aren't easier for any other parent. But they are clear and understandable. Being a great front-seat coach means embracing the same behaviors that great business leaders use to bring out the best in their team.

How and where you use them, can vary. But use them.

On the way to the event
When a child is on the way to practice, you may be able to offer encouragement and reinforce some key concepts. But if you've waited until a fifteen, twenty or even sixty-minute drive to their event to discuss approaches, philosophies, goals or areas of emphasis, it's too late. You won't be empathetic. You won't focus on rewards. You will focus on tactics and lessons that won't be learned. Those are the conversations that need to take place at home, away from the immediacy of forthcoming efforts.

Sitting in the backseat, preparing for practice, the last thing they need is a screaming parent making them anxious by telling them to be calm. It simply doesn't work, and any such efforts will either be ignored or have a negative impact on performance.

Instead, try one of these approaches:

1) Focus on long-term goals. Like we said, drawing up a plan twenty minutes before a game is futile, but talking about their personal goals – maybe those your son outlined before the season – is productive. Explore whether your son has adjusted his, or if they remain the same. Don't connect the topic of the conversation to that specific practice or game, just explore bigger picture themes. It may actually shift their perspective on the events at hand.

2) If you want to talk about the sport on other levels, pick a tangent. For example, if you watched a professional soccer game over the weekend, breakdown the performance of a particular athlete you watched. Describe plays that you admired and help model visualization techniques. The topic

is still soccer related, but you're not focused on your child's performance.

3) Consider moving away from sports and focus on school or academics. There's a plethora of topics here. If possible, you can even use this time to assist with homework, given some level of adeptness at verbal instruction.

4) How about friends? Do you know what's going on in your son or daughter's social life? The people with whom they surround themselves will have as much or greater an impact that any one coach, team or practice session. Use your time together to learn about those friends. If you happen to be driving your child's teammate(s), it's even more appropriate to ask about social topics. Ask the teammate(s) about their friends as well.

5) With all of your emphasis on sports, have you considered that your child may have other overlooked interests? Is there a burning desire to write, paint or play an instrument? Does your daughter want to start a small business because she's fascinated with learning the mechanics of entrepreneurship? Each endeavor could become as or more useful than athletics in its own right. There's no reason such pursuits can't be born in the backseat of a car headed to the soccer field. Again, these are also great topics if you happen to be carpooling with teammates.

Great front-seat coaches can have a dramatic impact on how their children feel when they step onto the field. They may not always talk, instead choosing to let them rest. But when they do, they find topics unrelated to sports. Or, at very least, unrelated to the upcoming sports activity. Play that role and help your young athlete maximize his experience.

On the way home from the event

Maintaining the right mentality is even *more critical* after a game or practice on a car ride home. Young athletes are exhausted, emotional (in one way or another) and likely in need of time to cool down mentally and physically.

Parents are also emotionally geared up because they expended energy as a fan. That's fine, but the energy needs to remain on the sidelines of the field and not make its way into the car.

If you think your child was anxious heading to a game, wait until you see the collection of emotions after a tense contest. Yes, of course they will vary depending on the outcome. And, yes, this is the time to demonstrate the aforementioned empathy if something went wrong. Let your son know you love him unconditionally, even if he turned in a bad performance.

It's also the time for the rewards and recognition if your daughter's team won and she played well. Remember to focus on the passion and drive that got her to that point.

After that, it's recharge time. She probably won't want to break down the specifics of the game and you shouldn't urge that. Just let her decompress.

But again, those two stages may occur within thirty or forty-five minutes after the ride starts, which gives you plenty of time to talk about other things.

The pre-game approach makes sense post-game as well. Focus on the topics outlined above. But there are additional alternatives worth exploring.

1) If you want to stick with sports, look forward to future events, instead of immediately reflecting backwards. Maybe

the team won, but your daughter played poorly. You can immediately help her erase that memory by focusing on how exciting it will be to go into the next game on a hot streak.

2) Maybe the game provided a platform to discuss some of the life lessons in this book. As long as you can explore them without too much scrutiny on your child's performance, it's worth a shot. For example, your daughter tried a new technique she had just learned two days prior. It didn't work out, but she was comfortable making a mistake. Praise the effort!

3) Move into the future of your day as well. Let's your child know you look forward to whatever you have planned next. Maybe that's ice cream. Maybe it's dinner. As long as you're emphasizing something unrelated to soccer and making it clear how much you enjoy spending time together, it's a great topic. It will remind her that your love is not related to outcomes on the field.

4) For that matter, plan something post-game to ensure there's quality non-drive time on the schedule. If you don't already have something in the works, use drive time to talk about making plans together.

Wait to give the feedback

No matter what approach you choose, there's one rule every parent should embrace: don't immediately give detailed feedback about your child's on-field performance.

Everyone makes mistakes (see Chapter Three). It's how we learn. And this is the critical way to make sure growth occurs. When that happens, bite your tongue and just focus on driving your child home after a tough game.

People most often know when they mess up in the rest of life also. Not always, but frequently. It may not be as blatant as letting the game-winning goal roll between your legs, or leaving your girl unmarked just before that. But, there's a good chance your daughter figured out that she messed up. She doesn't need her dad to tell her immediately following the error. She already feels bad about herself.

Instantaneously piling on criticism may actually worsen the situation. It can generate an emotional response that stunts the growth of your child.

In other words, *wait to give* feedback.

The password test

There are many ways we, as parents, are bad front-seat coaches in everyday life. And all of them need to stop.

One day, Kendall came from school and told us our passwords for various online accounts – including bank account access – were average to below average. It was a very unexpected but assertive proclamation.

How did she know that?

In school, we were talking about how insecure internet passwords are. Our teacher mentioned that you can visit certain website to test password strength. So, while we had some free time, we looked up the sites she mentioned and started entering passwords to see what the site would say.

Panic immediately set in, and Kendall could tell instantly based on our body language and changed demeanor. What information had she given this website? How did she know it was secure? Had our privacy or identity been compromised accidentally?

The questions immediately commenced, with rapidity and intensity.

By the time the barrage ended, two things were crystal clear: Kendall hadn't done any irreparable harm, but she knew she had made a mistake. It was very apparent to her. She had really, really screwed up (or potentially done so) without even realizing it.

Kendall felt horrible immediately.

As we continued to try and dissect what had happened, just to double check that she hadn't divulged critical personal information, the tears began to flow. Not only did she know she did something wrong, she had begun to beat herself up more as we began to worry less.

That's when the lessons from this chapter kicked in. She had figuratively just come off the field after a bad game. There was absolutely no reason to pile on analysis and criticism. Breaking down her mistake further at that moment would have deepened an already excruciatingly painful wound.

By letting it go and letting her interpret and deal with the mistake at hand, she was able to recharge and rebound. Time helped heal the wounds. Kendall's emotions ran their course and within hours, we were able to sit on the couch and discuss the situation in greater detail. Less upset, she was able to listen to our explanation of why it had scared us. We were able to explain what dangers could have come about from her actions. It became a teachable moment, instead of one charged purely with emotion and frustration.

In this situation, we were able to apply the same care, concern and caution used when letting Kendall unwind in the car after a game. This time we were letting her unwind after a mistake made at school. But we leveraged the same framework needed by a good front-seat coach.

As the evolved front seat-coach, you give your child leadership in the form of:

- *your ear*
- *your empathy*
- *rewards and recognition*
- *space to recharge*
- *plenty of information*
- *fairness*

…as part of that ride to the game, home from the game or to any practice. That's the job and the best thing you can truly do as a chauffeur who becomes a great front-seat coach. Remember, it occurs in all walks of life.

Front-Seat Coaching Actions
It would be easy to say, "just don't front-seat coach." But when the reality of emotional intervention is such an obvious obstacle, it's easier to arm yourself with actions that empower you to be a *good* front-seat coach. Here are five things to consider.

1. Review the previous chapter and become a great chauffeur. Yes, there's much more to be done with drive time than remaining silent. But if you start with empathy, rewards/recognition and recharging, then just embrace silence, you'll be better off than a front-seat coach. Be a great chauffeur before you tailor the rest of your front-seat persona.

2. Practice silence. This may be the toughest behavior to embrace, but potentially the most important. When you're a silent front-seat coach, that's when your child can recharge. This is a critical action for you to take.

3. Make a list of the non-sports items you don't get to talk about with your child. Whatever ends up on that list, choose one for every drive and make it a topic of conversation.

4. Study a craft (sports, job roles, etc.) enough to talk about it on a macro-level. If it's soccer, be prepared to talk about professional athletes and their exploits. If it's graphic design your child loves off the field, learn about a few great designers. Either way, study so you can speak from a place of more authority.

5. Remind yourself before and after games to reward the right behaviors. No matter the outcome of a game, if you're telling your son that you're proud of his passion and drive, you're reinforcing big picture lessons.

Part Two:
On the Field

*(Impacting How the Game
is Played)*

Chapter Six:
Note Everyone Scores Goals

September 25th

Dear Diary,
I messed up the other day. Actually, I've been messing up for a while, but didn't realize it. It's really obvious that Kendall's coach values goal scorers over anything else. Like, a lot. Even if a player is severely challenged in other aspects of the game, but she possesses a bit of speed and the desire to score, she's going to play. Much more than anyone else.

Favoritism towards these types of players has definitely impacted Kendall. Those are the kids that take her playing time.

Since I noticed the trend, I've been encouraging her to try and score more goals. Bribery has been involved! It worked once, when she was eight years old. She earned tons of money for scoring goals. So, I thought it would work again and then maybe her coach would prefer her over some of her teammates.

But it hasn't really helped. And when we were talking about it – fortunately, we waited to have this discussion until after the car ride – it was clear that the financial incentive upset her.

Yeah, it made her feel more pressure. But not because she doesn't think she can score. More so because she doesn't really want to score. She sees herself as a great passer who helps other kids score the goals. In fact, she absolutely LOVES passing. It makes her really happy. She prefers passing over scoring every time. And every time I encouraged her to score instead of pass, she felt like I didn't appreciate the very thing that makes her special. Oops.

Boy did that hurt to hear. It forced me to do some serious soul searching. I mean, why did I care if she scores goals so much? After all, there are eleven kids on every team and games are usually 2-1. Not everyone scores! And it takes a team effort to win. She's always found a way to play and succeed, so I shouldn't be worried about it.

That's right. Not everyone scores. Kendall and I need to talk about that...

Sincerely,
Kent (aka, Soccer Dad)

Lessons learned on the field

So far, we've been talking about preparatory behaviors. General approach. Travel. Things like that. But, not about behaviors and lessons related to playing the game itself. There are rich experiences associated with both and it's time to start discussing some lessons from the field.

We've referenced observations made while hiding on the sidelines. One becomes very clear when you watch youth soccer games enough. This is going to shock you, but the coach has favorites. Some of the more progressive coaches favor kids that work hard and build great cultures. But, truly, that's unusual.

More likely, they favor kids that do flashy, cool stuff. NOTE: This is true in other sports also! The equivalent of scoring goals in baseball is hitting home runs. Or in football, it's throwing (or rushing for) touchdowns.

Sounds a lot like the rest of life, right? Remember the cavern between cool kids and nerds in school? Those that were "more attractive" and "better dressed" trended on the popular side. Those that got good grades, not as much. In recent years, this trend has shifted somewhat. Nerds have become cool, for instance. But, even still, popularity and favoritism require some level of self-promotion.

Athletes who self-promote tend to find favored footing. How do they promote? By scoring goals even if they should have passed. Or taking a risk that will, if successful, lead to glory. Even if failure hurts the team. It's a life lesson that can be taken from the field and applied to other aspects of life. This chapter, however, is not about self-promotion. In fact, that's not at all the life lesson on which we want to focus. Instead, we want kids to value what makes them uniquely special. We want them (and you, esteemed parent) to be comfortable with that idea that not everyone scores goals. And, not only is that ok, but it's actually awesome. You don't have to shamelessly self-promote. You should, instead, just be you.

Winning Versus Development
In youth sports in the United States, there is far too great an emphasis put on winning at far too young an age. It's incredible really. You see parents screaming their heads off at ten-year-old girls based on the score of game that is ultimately meaningless.

This has, in the opinion of many pundits, had a catastrophic impact on the way we develop young athletes in this country. But, that's an entirely different topic, for a different book, for a different day. From the perspective of a soccer dad trying to find life lessons from the sidelines, however, it's also quite illuminating.

This early emphasis on winning dramatically inhibits development. That may seem counterintuitive to some people. The better athletes who are developing more rapidly have a direct impact on the outcome of a game, right? Not necessarily.

The outcomes of a youth soccer game are often determined by sheer physical prowess – the tallest, strongest and fastest kids. They may not be the most skilled, nor the most interested in becoming skilled, but for some time they are capable of dominating games just because they have more athletic tools. Possibly (probably, even) because they are ahead of their peers on the growth curve.

Coaches put those kids in starring roles and, often, they have immediate success. They do push smaller kids around, they do run faster and as a result, they do score goals. Subsequently, their teams win. That makes the coach look like a genius to parents most concerned with outcomes. Parents are happy, jobs are safe.

Wash, rinse, repeat.

The related oversight

Something almost sinister is going on behind the scenes, however. Let's take two different athletes who are fictional composites of dozens of athletes we've watched play with and against Kendall over the years.

While Anna is the biggest, tallest, fastest kid on the team, she is being featured by the coach and made a "star." She doesn't really work on the nuances of the game. In the case of soccer, that means improving technical prowess, tactical awareness and soccer IQ. She can score, so no one asks her to pass. Or play defense, too much. She stands around when she doesn't have the ball. But the goals erase any negativity.

Meanwhile, Isabella is a late-bloomer. She's five inches shorter, thirty pounds lighter and a bit slower than Anna; primarily because her legs are shorter, and her muscles aren't yet developed. No one knows this yet, but Isabella will actually be taller, stronger and faster than Anna in five years.

Regardless, on this ten-year-old soccer team, she's overlooked. While Anna's physical dominance puts her at the top of the coach's list, Isabella works relentlessly on her craft. She becomes more technically proficient with each passing day – mastering sophisticated and challenging footwork. She studies the game and understands the "right way" to play.

However, it doesn't translate to goals. Because she is smaller than other kids, she has to rely on quickness. And Isabella excels at a number of subtle things such as passing, team defense and more. No, she doesn't feel comfortable running other kids over or arbitrarily initiating physical contact. That doesn't mean she lacks aggression – she just uses it in different places while Anna will run kids over (then stand around waiting for the ball to come back to her).

While she is systematically building an unmatched tool set for use on the soccer field, her coach and the parents focus on girls like Anna who are producing goals – if nothing else – and immediately visible results.

To the trained eye, Isabella isn't completely overlooked. Every time she is on the field, her team performs better than it does when she isn't on the field. The passing is cleaner, the communication is better, and the defensive approach is more reliable.

The team wins when she is in the game. But few people appreciate her impact. Even the coach doesn't fully appreciate her contributions, because she doesn't score goals.

Soccer is a team game. Plain and simple. In a typical game (between sixty and ninety minutes, depending on the age group) there may be only a handful of goals scored. A high-scoring game is 4-2. So, if only six goals are scored by four or five different players, what is everyone else doing? And why aren't we more focused on all of that stuff?

Not everyone scores goals

Isabella's story – in the soccer world and in the rest of life – is typical. In a pop culture society, we are attracted to flash. Goals, speed and power are all flash. But the reality is that not *everyone scores goals*. And that doesn't make a player who isn't scoring goals less valuable. Quite the contrary. It makes her a critical piece of the team dynamic that can ultimately propel your group to immeasurable heights.

Early in a young athlete's career, it's easy to discourage that mentality because so much value is put on the flash.

Consider this simple question: can any player score goals alone? To some extent, yes. But at some point, defenses will learn how to shut down a selfish player, regardless of athletic prowess. When that happens, the rest of the team is needed.

The girls that play defense and can win the ball.
The girls that move to create space for their teammates.
The girls that have vision and can pass with fluency.

These are individual skills that ensure a *team* can reach a point of excellence. These are the skills that help maximize a goal scorer and bring a winning culture to your team. And they are the skills that can make a player special in her own right.

Not everyone scores goals. Not only is that ok, it's necessary. It's something that should be celebrated and appreciated. In a team sport, the emphasis on team-oriented contributions must be the focus of reward.

If your daughter is a great passer, celebrate her great passes. And don't worry about the goals she may or may not score.

If your daughter is a great defender, celebrate the stops she makes on the opposing team. And don't worry about the goals she may not score.

Not everyone scores goals. Find what makes your child special, and ensure it's appreciated. By appreciating those skills, consider the impact you're actually having.

Your daughter feels seen.
Your daughter feels appreciated.
Your daughter feels confident.
Your daughter feels like the passion and drive are worth it.
Your daughter will have more fun knowing her efforts are understood.
Your daughter will believe.

Isn't that more worthwhile than bribing her to score some goals?

Not everyone gets the solo

Hayden's dance offers a platform to explore this issue as well. Dancers' work typically manifests itself in some type of performance. Maybe it's a competition. Maybe it's a recital. Maybe it's both. Either way, there's usually a show. That is, after all, what performers live for: performances.

At a given dance studio, there may be dozens of classes. The number of students in a class varies, but it's always more than one. Maybe it's three, ten or twenty. But in any situation, it's enough that instructors, when the time comes to choreograph recital or competition routines, have to make choices.

Who will be featured? Where do the kids stand in the formation? *Who will have a solo in the middle of the routine?*

If there are twelve dancers in one routine, not everyone can be front and center. Not everyone can get the critical solo. And not all want it, either. Many kids are happy staying out of the spotlight and taking their place within the troupe as a supporting dancer.

While everyone watches the soloist, the troupe keeps the routine going. It gives the number texture and depth. The other dancers, if choreographed correctly, actually highlight the soloist as well. They are incredibly important.

How many times have you watched a dance solo and thought, within ten seconds, that it was boring? At that point you give up and tune out. But, in a group number, even if there are solos to watch, there is so much going on that you remain intrigued and entranced. Each dancer, if only for a moment, does something critical to make the routine work overall. Those dancers earn your attention, one at a time. If, by the end, you realize the number was great, you may be able to point out a dancer or two to that excelled. But you can also recall the contributions of many other dancers in "the back" who brought the routine to life.

Not everyone needs a solo to matter. Just like we need to celebrate soccer players that don't score goals, so too must we celebrate dancers that don't solo. Those that are anchoring the back row to make sure the show has a sense of depth and complexity. An individual that stands out can be beautiful. But she alone doesn't fill the room. And not every dancer that fills a room will have a solo, either.

Maximize the talents of every player

Isabella's story happens every day off the field as well. We so often emphasize the need to be leaders. Kids are taught that they should learn to lead. Because that's the aspiration, teachers focus on the equivalent of the fastest, strongest and most aggressive students. The ones that comply and get good grades. They score goals, or in the school setting, ace tests and projects.

This too is a mistake. Yes, the excellent students (the visible accomplishments) are absolutely important players in the academic landscape. But school is about learning for the purpose of application, right? You acquire tools for use in the real-world, whatever that may be for you. The best test-takers do not necessarily translate to the most successful leaders or impactful members of a team. They aren't always the best creators, the best managers, the best designers or the best builders.

As your daughter pursues a passion for robotics or video game design or baking, she needs to also know that not everyone scores goals in those endeavors. Most great pursuits require extraordinary teamwork and there are numerous roles to be played on every team.

Consider that her ambition may translate to pursuing a career in those disciplines. After all, that's the reason you learn, to have the tools to forge a chosen path. If only focused on "scoring goals," your child will miss so many other ways to successfully contribute in these areas. How can you equate this life lesson learned on the soccer field to that interest area? Let's use the robotics example. If your daughter wants a career in that field of work, is her only option to become the inventor? Of course not. There are so many other paths.

Build world class products or services
Market a value proposition that will stand out
Sell big deals
Deliver exceptional customer service
Innovate and do it all over again

There are a number of roles to be played in the business continuum. Every company has these big-ticket tasks to take on, and that's if you just move to the obvious roles that fall outside of *inventor*. Consider the less glamorous counterparts to those tasks listed above that are often overlooked in the spectrum of opportunity.

Build world class products or services.
Then manage them to operational efficiency to ensure they are profitable.
Market a value proposition that will stand out.
Then write compelling and error-free copy for an annualized digital campaign calendar.
Sell big deals.
Then review the price to ensure it's appropriate and review the contracts to ensure the company is protected.
Deliver exceptional customer service.
Then document common user errors to create an FAQ and maximize efficiency.
Innovate and do it all over again.
Build that innovation into a responsible annual budget that still meets profitability standards.

Unless you're in a start-up scenario, the groups responsible for these sub-tasks are not the same people associated with the primary tasks.

Instead, they are less glamorous and less rewarded. But no less critical. And, typically, they are the first steps towards reaching business goals.

They are people in the finance department, content writers, contract coordinators, technical experts and more. They are Emma, not Anna. They don't score goals, but they certainly help the team win. Without them, the company would come to screeching halt every time the big deal was sold. Why? It would never get contracted, delivered, supported or managed.

As your child pursues robotics, encouraging her to be only the inventor or top sales person limits her ability to see and consider any number of valuable and fulfilling roles. Those may actually be the focus of her passion and drive.

Watch a great soccer coach and appreciate how he handles the "role" players, or even just the less glamorous contributors. Tell your daughter to watch and appreciate it and consider how it can and will apply to other pursuits in the future. Conversely, watch the blatantly prejudiced coach and how he ignores or overlooks critical players making contributions. Ensure your daughter knows there is a better way. One that creates successful integration into a team culture. Have her embrace any role she takes on and work to become the best she can be at it. If she wants to be a defender (or, in the business world, a project manager) encourage her to be the best at it and be unique.

Not Everyone Scores Goals Actions
Wanting the spotlight is natural. It's an easy way to feel accepted, appreciated and adored. So many aspire to take on the leading role. As a society, we don't place enough value on the less visible jobs that carry as much meaning and substance. Sadly, glamourizing a few specific actions and ignoring those that perform important work starts at places like the youth soccer field. There are many ways to

emphasize the importance of those who don't score goals. Here are some actions to put this behavior into practice.

1. Identify and discuss all of the roles on a team. Dive deep into how each on contributes to the group's overall success. You and your child have to know and understand the importance of everyone – goals scorers and beyond – to combat the notion that only one person is important.

2. Explore the types of contributions that make your son happy. What does he believe his special gift is on the playing field? If it's scoring goals, that's great! But maybe he loves to pass, or he wants to be a goalkeeper. In other sports, consider the same questions. In school, also take this approach. If he loves art, or math, or social studies understand why and embrace how those skills can make him a unique and critical contributor to various groups.

3. Celebrate the accomplishments of everyone, even the least visible contributors. As a parent, modeling this behavior will let your child know that you mean what you say and that you truly value those with the more subtle but important roles. Two things happen with this. First, your child will feel more comfortable stepping into roles to which he aspires. Second, he will become a better teammate by pointing out those contributions to others.

4. Actively discuss team dynamics in all walks of life. Ensure you're seeking a deeper understanding of the contributions of each team member, regardless of the setting. This type of cross-training will benefit your daughter on and off the field.

5. Reflect on the various roles you've played throughout your life – either in sports, business, or the family. Go through the same exercise with your son. Are there patterns? Can

you demonstrate an ability to play different roles in different settings depending on the need? All too often we see the world through present circumstances but reflecting on the past helps you see options for the future.

Chapter Seven:
Know Your Position
(and Another)

October 2nd

Dear Diary,
It's really interesting to watch Kendall mature, both as an athlete and as a person. Where those two intersect is pretty compelling in its own right.

For the first few years she played sports, athleticism always seemed to win out. With her, with her teammates. Whomever. The fastest and strongest ones won. Now, at just eleven years old, it's pretty clear that the mental aspect of the game is catching up. The good athletes get beaten more and more often by the smart athletes. Which is also really interesting. And fun to watch.

It also means that Kendall and her friends have moved into a different period of growth. Being smart means so many different things. Awareness is a big part of that. You need to be prepared for what you are going to do with the ball before you get the ball. You need to understand what the other team is doing so you can adjust your position on the field.

The key thing that makes it possible is to understand the role each position plays on the field. When you're a defensive player, your job is different than when you're an offensive player. The speed and angles change based on where you play. As I watch, it's obvious even to me. It's also clear the girls are beginning to understand this.

So, that's the lesson to talk through with Kendall. Spend time being a student of the game, so she really knows her primary position. If she can grow in her awareness and knowledge of her position, she'll be a smarter player.

The next step, then, is to learn other positions so she can see the game from all different angles and also add value to her team. One thing at a time, but that's definitely the discussion for us to continue having.

Sincerely,
Kent (aka, Soccer Dad)

Where should I play?

Sitting in the grass as we watch soccer practices, parents see kids go through drills and then scrimmage. There always seems to be some version of that formula at each practice. One of the more interesting exercises is observing where coaches play your child (and other children) during the scrimmage.

Let's all be honest. At first, no one likes to play defense. So that can become a source of debate or frustration. No matter where you play, it's likely you'll complain about it at some point.

But someone has to play defense for the team to win. Great defenders are, in fact, a rare and valuable commodity. Team sports depend on players to execute well-defined roles at specific positions. On a field with eleven kids, each position is important and requires different skills, focus and preparation.

Once you accept that each position is critical to a team's success, it's important to treat each one as unique. It's important to recognize that learning the nuances of each position is like learning a different craft. This also provides children with outstanding life lessons.

All coaches deal with the position conundrum and may handle it very differently. But the approaches share common principles. Namely, all good coaches emphasize the need for their athletes to truly and deeply know the responsibilities of their position. The great coaches also continue to build depth and demand their players *know another position*.

Knowing your position

Exceptional athletes make the extraordinary look ordinary, no matter how high the degree of difficulty. Spend enough time watching your daughter's soccer practice, and you'll undoubtedly marvel at the athletic prowess of kids that haven't yet seen middle school hallways.

- A twenty-five-yard strike into the upper right-hand corner of the goal? *Check.*
- A diving save against all odds on the final penalty kick to win the championship game? *Check.*
- A twenty-yard recovery run and tackle to stop a last-second breakaway goal? *Check.*

Many soccer parents are nodding their head at the recollection of these or very similar moments. Kids can really amaze you.

But watch closely. For every insane athletic miracle, there are four, five or six simple contributions that led to that moment. On a well-coached team, everyone knows her position. Players are taught to execute it and such success leads to the seemingly unexpected breakthrough.

That twenty-five-yard strike into the upper right-hand corner of the goal started two (or four, or six!) passes earlier. The left winger recognized that the opponent had committed its defense to her side, so she quickly passed the ball underneath (backwards) and simultaneously communicated with her teammate to make one more pass to the midfielder who felt comfortable taking the shot from twenty-five yards away because the defense hadn't yet recovered, and she saw the goalkeeper off her line. Two teammates understood their job, executed it and made it possible for the team to succeed, culminating in one individually executed task.

The winger did her job. The midfielder did her job. And the striker did her job. Just as it was designed. By knowing the nuances of their positions, they took "ordinary" steps that culminated in an extraordinary play.

It's in the details
Great team moments, derived from disciplined individual play, only occur when players truly know the specifics of their position. The

formula is similar in all team sports and provides a great paradigm for team participation in other walks of life – a research team, debate club, rock band or dance troupe. Emphasizing three core concepts will help inculcate the right approach to learning a position, and then another.

1. **Position(ing)**: They call it a "position" for a reason. Typically, there are set places on the field, court, etc., where your child needs to be when he plays a specific role. But, those names are most often associated with the *starting* place for your child's position. After that, your son has to figure out where to be in different situations during a game. Understanding the true nuances means developing a full awareness of where to be when the ball and other players are at specific points on the field, offensively and defensively. Where should your son be when he has the ball and doesn't have the ball, and so on. How should that be modified at any particular point in the game. Focus on position(ing).

2. **Skill Emphasis**: Yes, there are basic skills every athlete needs in every sport. But different positions require certain skills to be more developed than others. Strikers score goals, so one might think they need the strongest foot. But, most strikers score goals inside the six and eighteen-yard boxes. Mexican striker Javier Hernandez, better known as Chicharito, notched his forty-third goal in the English Premier League during the 2017-2018 season while playing for West Ham United (he had previously played for Manchester United). All forty-three goals had come from within the eighteen-yard box. Not a single one had come from "outside the box." That means they are close to the goal, and typically placing the ball in the corner after receiving a pass and making a quick turn. Pace, movement,

accuracy and turns all have premium value over ball velocity for a striker.

3. **Situational Awareness**: What are your daughter's responsibilities in specific situations? Time is a great example. Say her team is up by one goal with just ten minutes left to play. She's a deep-lying central midfielder, typically asked to initiate the offense from deep in her own half, or maybe in the middle-third of the field. Her strengths include switching the point of attack and delivering aerial balls over the top of the opposing defense for attackers to run under. Those skills are extraordinarily valuable to the team, but less so when it has a one-goal lead with ten minutes remaining. In that case, it's the right time to drop deeper, focus on defensive tactics, and play shorter passes to safely retain possession. The task would be different as a striker. In the same scenario, a striker would need to understand his role. But everyone's situation will dictate a slightly different approach to the game at different times. If everyone knows her position, the team will be better at all turns.

Great moments don't often happen by accident. And they aren't always the product of superhuman individual effort. Instead, they frequently result from a group of individuals who execute each aspect of their positions correctly in a given situation.

Does that sound like it applies to other scenarios also? More on that in a bit.

(And another)
So, you've helped your son learn his position. Guess what? It's time to go through the same process again. A great team doesn't limit players to knowing just one position. Spend enough time on a soccer field and you realize how often coaches forget to teach their kids a

second (or third) position.

Specialization shouldn't happen by the time kids are eleven, but it does. First, it's at the sport-level. *If you want to continue playing on (this) the top team, at (this) an elite club, you really have to stop playing other sports. If you don't, you'll fall behind.*

Never mind that all research says early specialization is a bad idea. It makes kids more injury prone. It stymies balanced developed of various motor skills and coordination types. Oh, and it makes a sport more like a job than fun. Remember fun? If not, review Chapter One.

Coaches have seen and read this research but they either don't respect it or, more likely, don't care. Youth sports is big business and the more you get top talent to commit to your club and pay its bills, the more successful you'll be. In order to maximize those athletes and get those wins, coaches require "commitment" at all times. As a result, sports specialization comes first.

Then, positional specialization follows close behind.

I know you played midfield, striker and back the last few years. But, on this team, you're going to be a left wing and we'll focus your development at that position. I am going to give you a very specific job, and that's all I want you to do. Nothing else.

To be blunt, this is stupid and also inhibits both player and team growth. It also detracts from one of the key life lessons your son should be taking away from the soccer field – he will be a better team member if he knows his position, and also another, on any team of which he is a member. Period.

Short-term thinking
No matter what they say, coaches limit your child's opportunity to

learn and play multiple positions for two simple reasons – and neither have anything to do with the long-term benefit of youth athletics or development.

1. **It's easier**: When they can slot young athletes into specific positions, it makes the life of a coach easier. Why? Because they can reduce the number of moving parts significantly. They know they can save time by grouping kids together positionally, and then maximizing their talents in those specific roles.

   In fact, it's the wrong approach for a few reasons. First, it stunts the development of the athletes. At ten, eleven or twelve years old, it's impossible to know where on a playing field each athlete will ultimately thrive.

   That evolution often continues well after a player has reached the top of her sport as well. Julie Ertz, a professional soccer player for the Chicago Red Stars and United States Women's National Team (USWNT) folk hero for her performance during the 2015 World Cup winning team, continues to go through positional changes. During her college years, she was an attacking midfielder for the Santa Clara Broncos. She broke into the USWNT team starting lineup as a center back, making the successful conversion to defense. Then, in 2017, she pushed forward to become a defensive midfielder both at the National Team level and for the Red Stars.

   Her attacking midfield prowess married perfectly with her experience defensively to make the transition smooth. But consider for a moment that she was a starting center back and widely considered one of the most valuable players during the World Cup victory run. Framed differently, she was one of the best players in the world. And yet, she continued to learn and play other positions.

Julie continued to evolve. As USWNT head coach Jill Ellis sought a more complete, dynamic starting lineup she didn't settle on Ertz as a defender because it was easier.

So, why should a youth coach treat kids any differently? They do. And if you see a coach taking the easy way out, make note.

2. **It helps them win:** Because positional focus simplifies their life, it helps youth coaches focus on winning. Running a team of twenty kids is hard work. You're responsible for developing effective and impactful training for two or three sessions each week. If done correctly, you're tending to the varied needs of different personality types. On game day, coaches need to send their best lineup onto the field, balance playing time and find the right intersection of competition and development. It's a lot to ask and it's time-consuming, overwhelming and often controversial.

   As we've already explored, winning is far too often the ultimate focus at the youth level. So, as a coach balances out the varied competing forces, she also seeks to reduce variables to win games. When you slot kids into a particular position, it may not maximize talent development. But it can help maximize the short-term impact of that talent. It allows the coach to get closer to a winning product, faster.

Short versus long-term

Ultimately, positional specialization is a short-term strategy. The best youth coaches understand this and will sacrifice winning for the longer-term gain. Kendall had a club coach, Jeremy, who understood this.

Yes, he loved to win. Sure, he had positional *preferences* for his players. But he also understood that making kids learn multiple positions made them better as a whole.

If a girl's skill set made her most appropriate for a midfielder role, she would most often play there. But during a game where the team needed to mix things up – maybe they were struggling – that girl would find herself playing forward or defense. Jeremy wasn't avoiding the challenge of teaching them on the fly. In fact, he was embracing it.

He knew that sometimes a short-term loss had significant long-term gains, both for the child and for the team. There were five key ways Jeremy's philosophy benefits the development of youth athletes.

1. **Perspective**: When your son is forced to learn another position, he will see his preferred position from a completely different perspective. If he typically sits in the midfield and waits for his backs to feed him the ball, he becomes predisposed to certain movements or patterns on the field. Taking a turn as an outside back makes him realize how challenging it may be to complete certain passes. Then, when he returns to midfield, he can adjust his own approach to help his teammates.

2. **Preference**: A player's skill, as demonstrated during training sessions, may suggest she's best suited to play midfield. But she may think like a striker and thrive more in game situations at that position. By taking the time to develop a second (or third) position, coaches may stumble into a better fit for an athlete.

3. **Communication**: Similarly, your daughter may begin to appreciate different challenges associated with another role. For example, it is difficult to see oncoming defenders from

the weak side of the field. As a midfielder, playing back, she gets a sense of when it's most critical to communicate defensive movements. When she returns to her midfield role, she'll be more prone to communicate with teammates to help them avoid problems.

4. **Big Picture**: Quite simply, players that know another position will have a stronger understanding of the tactics that dictate action in a soccer game. If team members understand what others must do, there's a greater chance they will work in harmony.

5. **Depth**: We touched on this above. Teaching players multiple positions gives coaches (and teams) a backup plan. If someone gets hurt, the team has more options to replace her. Depth ensures continuity when things don't go as expected. And everyone need to plan for the unexpected as often as possible.

Applying the concepts off the field

The concepts we've explored – both learning your position and another – are certainly applicable for your child off the field. Great team players and leaders alike leverage these concepts to ensure maximum performance in various situations. Let's breakdown one example where knowing both her position and others uniquely equipped Kendall for academic success.

Remember school science fairs? They still exist, but now they are called STEM (Science Technology Engineering and Math) contests. During middle school, Kendall became a regular participant.

Her events differed from traditional science fairs in a few key ways. The most obvious was the nature of the activities. Instead of building a bridge or protecting the shell of an egg during a fall, students were asked to use connectable toys to build complex structures with thematic meaning (sustainability, for example). It was small-scale engineering at its finest.

The STEM contests were also team-based. One year, Kendall was on a team of five, the next year she was one of four participants. Their projects were interesting, but the team dynamics are the piece that warrant review. In truth, that was the focus of nearly all conversations surrounding the contest anyway.

After returning from school, we'd often talk about her progress on the STEM project. Of course, she would describe the tactical progress. Outline the concept of their creation – particularly as it fit within the directions, rules or requirements. Kendall would talk about why she liked the team's project and whether or not she felt it had a chance to win an award at the competition.

But most of her time was actually spent talking about the team and how it worked together. She would characterize the different roles her teammates were playing. One boy was the *de facto* project manager. Another boy did a great job obtaining and organizing materials. One girl would manage quality control, testing parts as they were built. Kendall found herself in a "jack of all trades" role, that entailed helping each teammate complete his job, reflecting on the macro-level vision and ensuring the project was on track.

Kendall had tremendous ability to articulate each person's role, and how they contributed to team success. She also saw where they had a surplus or lack of ability. She learned the value of her role, then, as a generalist. And, in doing so, made sure to learn not just one other role, but multiple roles.

When she participated during sixth grade, a faculty advisor commented that "the team worked incredibly well together, problem-solving and working as one." It was a chemistry the team had developed by collaborating for nearly four months. They had developed, prototyped and tested their concepts daily. When the time came to enter their contest, they thought they were ready.

At the final competition, things didn't go as planned and exceptional teamwork and problem-solving skills were needed to overcome some challenges. The team hadn't packed all of the materials for their design – one they had been working on for months. Without the tools to execute their vision, the group adjusted in real-time. It didn't even strike Kendall as being that unique – the team worked within the roles they had adopted and took on other roles to get the job done. In the short amount of time given to recreate months of work, everyone had to complete multiple jobs to re-engineer, re-prototype and re-test their structure in just a few hours. Each team member worked with a big-picture perspective and situational awareness. They saw their playing field from multiple positions, which let them move quickly, together, as a unit.

It doesn't seem like a big deal, but the team was nominated for one of a just a few distinguished awards among a group of nearly eighty total teams. They didn't win, but they achieved significant recognition while redesigning their project in just a few hours. Something that had taken them months was still considered award-worthy after a rapid on-site redesign. That is a testament to how each one knowing multiple positions made the team better.

By the way, Kendall wasn't the only athlete on the team. Each of the other three members played at least two team sports. They had been unknowingly exposed to similar life lessons, even if they weren't explicitly taught.

Knowing your position (and another) will always make you capable of integrating with a team, regardless of the scenario. On the field, in the school room, or anywhere else.

Know Your Position (and Another) Actions

So often, we talk about being great team members or building high performing teams. But few people take the requisite steps to deliver on that promise. As part of sports team, your children have no choice but to immerse themselves in team dynamics. Knowing their position, and then another, ensures top performance. It's just part of the job. Even if the team isn't exceptional, there are lessons to be gleaned from daily participation. Here are some ways to identify and embrace these key behaviors.

1. Clarify two things: What position is your child playing and what position does she want to be playing? Are they the same? Are they different? It's important to have clarity on the role so it can be studied. If the position being played is different than the preferred position, that may not be such a bad thing, and we'll get to that momentarily. But know the answer to these two questions.

2. Study the position your child is playing carefully and completely, and help them do the same. Understand what is expected in terms of skills, tactics and approaches to the position. How does it most often help a team? How does it most often hurt a team? Help your child become a practitioner.

3. After your child has studied and learned the specifics of her position, have her learn another. If she came up with two different positions going through the first action, you already know what position to study next – the one she wants to be playing. If she isn't sure what to study, choose a position that she interacts with and on which she is often dependent. Help her learn that one.

4. Develop specific exercises to help your daughter master the various components of positional play. This will be different

116

for every position on every type of team – but there will certainly be physical and mental components. Break them down and ensure your daughter is training each part appropriately.

5. Put it all together. Take a step back and help your daughter appreciate how improving her positional aptitude has improved her overall understanding of the team dynamic. Have her talk to coaches and teammates about it, and suggest she aspire to elevate the team's approach to positional awareness. Everyone that functions better as an individual within the context of the whole will be pushing the team to new heights.

Chapter Eight:
Play Ninety Minutes
(and Expect Extra Time)

October 9th

Dear Diary,

It's really impressive watching these kids commit themselves to playing sports at such a young age. I know you have tons of energy when you're young. But, wow, it must be exhausting. They practice for ninety minutes, two or three times a week, then play a few games on the weekend. When they aren't practicing with the team, they often do extra training on their own, with friends or at a professional facility.

It's intense!

Which makes it completely understandable that on some game days, these kids actually get tired. In so many cases, young athletes don't distinguish between the importance of practice and games. Which is the right approach. After all, they should just focus on improvement.

But seeing the cycle of perpetual motion, you realize there's a chance to talk about why you practice. Discuss the purpose of repetition. So, you're prepared for a game.

And if you prepare for the games, you don't need to worry about actual performance. Everyone is going to make mistakes. That's how they grow. When at all possible, however, they should make sure the games get the most energy. Young athletes should start to recognize that practice is building toward games. Fitness is building toward games. So, they should, at very last, give full effort for the entire game.

In the case of soccer, that means they should play ninety minutes with all of the effort and intensity they can offer. Taking that approach is a great lesson. It's the first way you get to teach kids that life is built on putting in work over a long period of time, with specific outcomes in mind.

That's this week's focus with Kendall. We'll talking about making sure to play ninety minutes with intensity.

Sincerely,
Kent (aka, Soccer Dad)

As Yogi used to say, it ain't over…

One of the oldest adages in sports is that you have to play to the end, because you never know what can happen. It's true in all walks life and you'll never see this more clearly than watching youth sports through a life-lessons lens.

Why does it matter? If you lived long enough, you've inevitably seen that things can change for better or worse on a dime. J.K Rowling, author of the *Harry Potter* novels, went from jobless to billionaire in just over a decade because she studied her craft and pursued her objective with passion, drive and diligence. She's the author of young adult fantasy novels, but when the chance came, she "left it all out on the field" of her choice.[9]

It happens much more quickly in sports. A soccer team can play terribly for eighty-nine minutes and be trailing by just one goal. Then, in the ninetieth minute, with the clock winding down, it grinds its way to an equalizer just because the players didn't give up. Tie game! Expecting extra time, the team had a bit of energy left and netted a game-winning goal three minutes into stoppage time. A complete turnaround, just because they played with intensity until the end.

That team may have played terribly all afternoon but playing a full ninety minutes kept them moving towards an objective.

This is such a clear and concise lesson, that it doesn't even need explanation. But we still want to provide a few illustrations. Soccer matches are ninety minutes. If you can get your team to play hard for ninety minutes, and even to expect extra time, you will build a high-performing group.

---

[9] Rachel Gillett, "From welfare to one of the world's wealthiest women — the incredible rags-to-riches story of J.K. Rowling," *Business Insider*, May 18, 2015, https://www.businessinsider.com/the-rags-to-riches-story-of-jk-rowling-2015-5.

In life, it may take more than ninety minutes of grind to reach a particular goal, but youth athletics can teach this critical lesson of perseverance, belief and continued ambition.

The "why" of how this works
So often, people give up. A team is losing, and it seems impossible to comeback. Some kids hate to lose – it's just how they are wired. But not all. And even the ones that hate to lose, well, they're kids, right? So eventually you may get to this point.

What does it matter? It's just a game.

Here's the thing, they're right. It's just a game. Ultimately, it's pretty meaningless as well. But, then again, you can say the same thing about life. It's all just a game, and no matter what we do, it's pretty meaningless in the long run. Right?

Unless you *make* it meaningful. Anything in life matters if you want it to, because it's your life. Youth sports gives you a great platform to explore and test that concept, and then arm your kids with the tools to make anything meaningful. To figure out where they want to play ninety minutes and some extra time, pursuing a desired result.

In Kendall's case, she had decided that sports were worth the effort. That meant giving maximum effort in training, practice and games.

For her younger sister, Hayden, dance and music were the chosen areas of passion. It may be easier for Hayden to give up if something goes wrong on a basketball court, because she's not committed to that pursuit. But on the dance floor, it's a different story. If Hayden fell out of a double-turn during competition, her version of playing ninety minutes would include digging deep to finish the choreography with perfection and precision for the remaining 120 seconds of her dance.

Extra time for a dancer could be selection to a dance-off, where Hayden would have a chance to redeem herself with a better overall performance. If she gives up, that isn't possible. If she plays the full ninety minutes (finishes her dance), there's a chance for redemption. Great things can happen.

Achieving their varied objectives requires an outlook that includes playing the full ninety minutes, dancing the entire 120 seconds or another specific commitment to an outcome. And because you don't know when the effort will produce that outcome, this behavior has to be consistently cultivated. Your child must play ninety minutes every time to achieve heroic end results. It won't pay off most of the time, but when it does, she'll be happy it did.

How it looks
Athletic outcomes are often based on skill (or lack thereof). But playing the full ninety minutes doesn't require specific athletic attributes. It doesn't require technical training. It just requires the desire to take on the challenge and the mental fortitude to see that challenge to its completion.

So how do you get to a point where this behavior becomes a consistent part of your approach? Watching your daughter or son's soccer practice or game, the ninety-minute athletes stand out rather quickly. And there are three attributes that they all possess. We'll list them here briefly, and then tackle them individually below.

1. *Belief.* When athletes play the entire ninety, they always think there's time to come back. Even when they are losing by a seemingly insurmountable goal total. Say, 5-1. The first trait of a ninety-minute athlete is the belief that playing until the end, no matter what the scenario, leads to positive outcomes.

2. *Grit.* Angela Duckworth, author and Professor of Psychology at the University of Pennsylvania, measured and defined grit in the context of entrepreneurs. The same concepts apply to athletes as well. When a girl plays all ninety minutes of a soccer game, grinding hard at the end of the game when the outcome looks dismal, coaches get a glimpse of grit.[10]

3. *Fitness.* Well-trained, fit teams win more games towards the end. Why? Because when most teams show signs of fatigue, fit teams know they have enough stamina to deliver their best performances at the end of the match. But that only happens if they play ninety and expect extra time, every game. Endurance is earned, not given.

It starts with belief
There are many words and phrases that could be slotted in here. *Resilience. Won't die attitude.* Whatever the case, watch players on a soccer field and you will see this characteristic clearly.

While most think it's inherent in the athlete, great coaches get this out of their players. The question is how. The answer? It's not complicated. It just requires communication and explanation. Great coaches tell their kids the value of playing until the end – outlining the benefits we've already touched on.

1. *The comeback.* Good coaches will share their personal comeback tales and make it clear to athletes that a comeback of miraculous proportions may always be in their future. It ain't over until it's over. Unless, of course, you quit. Then it's definitely over.

---

[10] Duckworth, Angela, *Grit: The Power of Passion and Perseverance* (New York: Scribner, 2016)

2. *The preamble.* So, your child's team plays to the end and still loses. Going full speed until the final whistle can establish a precedent for the next game or a re-match with the current team. This is where negative outcomes become the best introduction to future results. If you've ever participated in a team sport, you've probably experienced this phenomenon and understand how real momentum can be. Your child should take the chance to build momentum at every turn. Play a full ninety minutes and it can make the next ninety that much better.

3. *The case for improvement.* With the game out of hand, everyone gets a chance to make mistakes and improve. But that only works if your son is taking it seriously and going full speed. If his team is down 5-1 and there's just two minutes left to play, maybe he can work on that skill that has been challenging him. Or consider asking to play a different position. There's always something to work on. If he's going to spend time on the field, he should use it to the fullest.

Players must believe in that value of playing ninety. Give them the tools to do so.

Kendall's under-ten, or "U10" coach got this out of his team. It was one of the most unique groups that Kendall ever played with. The talent level was as diverse as you can imagine – the top girls were capable of playing elite soccer, the middle group was solid and the bottom third of the team cared dearly but lacked talent.

Magnus was a head coach with experience. He understood how to maximize the talents of each player. Even when the game went in the wrong direction, he would make an adjustment and the team's performance would change. During that U10 year, it seemed that he made such tweaks in every game. The team would often start slow, and then he would find a way to get them to emerge.

125

The slow starts, however, had an impact. Often, the team would put its best foot forward only after they fell behind. Sometimes by two or three goals. Comebacks are hard and digging in to work your way back takes a lot out of a team. So, it helps to have validation that they matter.

That's exactly what happened during one particular game early in that U10 season. The team had fallen behind by two goals, but Magnus got them to battle back. They cut the lead to one by the end of the first half. Then in the second half, they played with the same urgency and aggression early but couldn't score the goal needed to equalize. As the team started to look tired, a comeback seemed improbable. But Magnus urged them to fight, and with just about three minutes left, they finally tied the game. A win would take a superhuman effort, right?

Magnus didn't think so. He encouraged the girls to believe they could win. To attack the other team with the vigor needed to score and score quickly. His belief fueled the girls on the team. There was a renewed spark in their eyes and energy in their movements.

With just under one-minute left, the team took possession of the ball and began attacking down the sideline. The defense closed off passing lanes, so the one forward played it back to an outside back. That player, Kate, happened to have the ability to serve the ball right back into the attacking area of the field, which she did. Kate sent the ball high into the air, heading straight in the direction of the goal. It came down on the foot of the team's striker, named Corinne, who took one final shot. It hit the back of the net and the whistle blew just seconds later.

The team managed to make the nearly impossible happen by playing the full ninety minutes. They did again and again as the season went on. They won four more games that season in the last two or three minutes of play.

That group learned the value of playing ninety minutes and embraced it for the rest of the year.

Let's explore each of the components outlined above in greater detail.

Grit

Duckworth's concept of grit is based on an idea that some people succeed while others fail because of this one personality trait. She defines it as:

> .. *a combination of passion and perseverance for a singularly important goal—is the hallmark of high achievers in every domain.*[11]

In her research, this was the personality trait that most often separated successful entrepreneurs from those that failed. But one of her key findings was that grit can grow.

We've already emphasized the concept of passion together with drive earlier in this book. Connected to a goal, you're onto something. Why do those ideas have a place in this chapter? Because Duckworth's evolution of passion and perseverance into grit are often challenged in an adverse scenario where you must test yourself and continue.

That's what playing ninety minutes, regardless of the expected outcome at any point – five, twenty-five or eighty-five minutes in – is all about. Grit is harnessing passion and drive for ninety minutes. When a coach emphasizes grit on a soccer field – perseverance for a singularly important goal such as winning – that trait will grow when losses occur, so it can be flexed and leveraged into wins.

---

[11] Duckworth, Angela, *Grit: The Power of Passion and Perseverance* (New York: Scribner, 2016)

Duckworth associates entrepreneurial grit with the ability to overcome failure. You see this on the soccer field constantly. When the grittiest kids fail in some way, they simply figure out another way to succeed.

Kendall played with one girl who we'll call Sarah. Her game was the embodiment of grit. Her specialty was defense, which by very nature requires a high degree of grit. But her makeup was two parts athlete, one part soccer player, and seven parts grit. Sarah was the fastest girl on her team. Her soccer skills were good, but not exceptional. And yet, at a given time, she was one of the best players on the field. Why? Grit layered on top of athleticism.

Sarah would use her speed and instincts to pursue an opposing player. Often, she'd meet the girl she was marking at the same time the ball arrived. But just as frequently, she would misjudge, overplay or just get beat. What set Sarah apart, however, was that she viewed her misplay as the beginning, not the end. She worked harder to recover than she did to make the initial play. Sarah was gritty. She always played ninety minutes. She wanted extra time. It was a chance for her to take a risk, fail, and make it up all in the same thirty-second stretch.

Fitness
It's starts with a reason, a desire, an interest. But, to be sure, your child won't play ninety minutes at her fullest from day one. It's possible, but improbable. And even still, she will need to build up to being highly performant late in a game.

This requires a long-view. Once she's decided that playing ninety minutes is critical to her approach, she has to understand that it takes time. Each game, she gives as much as she can. At first, that may only be sixty minutes. Then sixty-five or seventy minutes. Play the full ninety minutes, just to finish the first time. The second time, pick up the tempo a bit at the end. The pattern continues until a team has pushed itself to peak performance. Add an element of endurance training to her protocol and there's a recipe for becoming a ninety-minute monster.

It will take time. But once it does, the ability to explore the avenues outlined above opens up in its entirety.

It also becomes a real competitive advantage. There will come a time when the other team gets tired because some teams do not emphasize playing until the end with the same vigor we're suggesting. When that happens, a comeback is within grasp because your daughter and her team will be playing with superior endurance. This only happens if fitness is emphasized in both winning and losing situations.

Mental toughness and physical preparation create athletes and teams that are ready to go the distance. When an athlete plays to the end, there's so much to be gained.

The ninety-minute life equivalent
Having trouble making the connection here? Playing the full ninety-minutes can teach your child (and you) so many valuable lessons about pursuing goals and overcoming adversity.

School is full of opportunities to apply this concept. The subject needs to matter to your children as they study. Maybe it's because they intrinsically like math or science or social studies. Maybe it's because they understand the value of education as a tool to accomplish various goals.

Once there is value associated with schoolwork, it's easy to translate the other components of playing ninety minutes. It takes grit – passion and perseverance – because mistakes are going to be made, and they will be discouraging. It takes fitness.

In this case, not necessarily physical, but mental endurance associated with long hours of study.

Persisting until the end of an assignment or test can bring about great results, even in the face of failure. Consider a physics exam, just ten questions long, that stumps your son for the first ten or fifteen minutes. He blanks on the formulas and methodologies required to complete the first three questions – he's already looking at a "C" before he even begins answering questions.

But he continues, knowing that even if that's his best grade, he can learn from his mistakes or build momentum for his next test. Doing the work will lead to improvement, after all.

By the middle of the exam, he's hit a groove. Questions four through eight are easier, and he moves through them quickly. His confidence builds, and he begins to remember the knowledge that evaded him early in the test. With time left to spare after finishing the tenth question, he moves back to the beginning of the test and works as quickly as possible to complete the first three questions.

Ultimately, the physics test didn't win. Your son earned a score of ninety-two percent, good enough for an "A" and in the top ten percent of his class. Why? Because he played the full ninety minutes. He understands the value of giving his effort until the end, and his belief paid off.

Can you see this working in other settings as well? Everything in life can benefit from committing to a full ninety minutes of play.

Play Ninety Minutes (And Expect Extra Time) Actions
Unlike many of the behaviors we've explored, playing ninety minutes translates very directly to the field and has an impact on the outcome of a game. It's also a relatively easy concept to discuss with your child. The challenge comes in translating the life lessons to other

disciplines. Use these actions to dive deep into the benefits of playing until the final whistle, regardless of outcome.

1. Talk about when the game ends. Seriously, does your child understand the rules of the game? It may seem rudimentary but unless they have a complete grasp of the box within which they're working, it's impossible to play on the edges or even move outside the box in any capacity. This is true in other facets of life as well.

2. Explore the benefits of playing to the end, regardless of perceived outcome. Particularly at a young age, it may not be clear how sustained effort can benefit the future. Outline the possibility of a comeback. Give examples.

3. Cross-training doesn't always have to be physical. Build a mental cross-training program for your child so he can truly learn about belief and grit. Identify people that embody such characteristics and explain why they are examples of these qualities.

4. Incremental improvement is the key to "playing ninety minutes" in a soccer game. Don't start with the end goal, but instead outline a means for your daughter to build up to quality effort for the entire game. Start at forty minutes, then build to sixty minutes, then eighty minutes, and eventually you'll land on ninety minutes or more.

5. Reflect on other areas of life where this concept has meaningful application. It starts with understanding what has meaning to your child – but when you've identified such an area, repeats steps one through four looking at a discipline or activity through that lens. A life lesson to be used anywhere!

Chapter Nine:
Play Fast

October 14th

Dear Diary,

Remember when a bunch of little kids moved up and down the soccer field in a pack? Every now and then, the ball would trickle out the side of that pack and the kids wouldn't even notice! Scoring wasn't really their objective and it was absolutely adorable to watch.

Those games didn't move very quickly, that's for sure. Yeah, they found a way to score goals, but sometimes it was after they had dribbled in a circle, or the wrong direction, or off the field completely.

That's really changed. Kendall's team plays fast. The girls run fast. They pass with pace. Everything is done with speed. In fact, coaches often say that's the biggest difference between top-level teams and other teams. The talent lets them play much faster. So, if you want to play with the best, some coaches will tell you, speed is the key.

Sure, I get it. But playing fast is a good lesson in life also. That's because playing fast is about two different things.

Yes, it's about physical speed. That's sort of obvious. To be fast, you have to work at it. Run extra sprints. Be sure you're practicing at full speed. All of that good stuff. Those are things you need to do in other parts of your life as well.

The second requirement to play fast is good decision making. You can't pass quickly unless you've already decided where the pass is going. And the fastest way to make that pass is to anticipate a situation and know your options.

In both cases, you also have to take some risks. Playing fast, doesn't always mean being right. But if you fail fast, you can fix it fast, right?

Speed – playing with speed – is about practice, preparation and risks. That's stuff Kendall can use forever.

Sincerely,
Kent (aka, Soccer Dad)

Speed kills in sports
That's the phrase. And it's mostly true.

Mostly. It's probably not as universal as some would lead you to believe. Speed isn't such a secret weapon in golf. No one deems you unstoppable for playing a round in a mere ninety minutes (keep in mind a typical round takes closer to four hours). The score is all that matters on the golf course.

We won't get into the debate surrounding golf as a sport.

But in other sports where you typically need to move past a defender with some level of purpose, it's good to be fast. It's even better to move with speed and skill at the same time. In soccer, they say technical speed is the promised land. United States Women's National Team star Mallory Pugh possessed such incredible technical speed at just eighteen years old, that she immediately impacted games at the highest level of competition when she burst onto the international scene.

Great coaches know that combined speed and skill is best. They seek it out and embrace it when they find it. Sometimes too much so, to the detriment of overlooking other positive qualities. However, when all other things are equal, speed is the variable that most impacts how the game is played. Watch enough youth soccer and you'll observe that, while other characteristics change, speed is always the trump card. The progression occurs in a few steps.

1. *Kids become more skilled.* At early ages, the more skilled a player is, the more she stands out. However, as children mature, their technical abilities become more uniform. Yes, there are outliers, including exceptionally technical players, and those that lack technical ability but still get by with speed or physicality. Overall, however, everyone is more skilled. So, then…

2. *The games become more organized.* Remember how much you laughed about five-year-old kids running up and down the field in a big bunch? Then how frustrated you got by kids kicking the ball downfield and chasing it? That mostly goes away. Passing and tactical prowess win out. Games sometimes feel like chess matches; at other times like boxing matches. But it all has a purpose. So, then…

3. *Everything gets faster.* The actions are completed faster. The tactical execution is done with more speed. Faster. Faster. Faster.

Yes, your son can have exceptional technical prowess and possess the ability to strike the ball equally well with both feet. Yes, he can see the field with unique vision that lets him know where your teammates will be even before they're in those spots.

Then speed differentiates. It trumps everything else. He needs to be able to move quickly, think quickly and react quickly. None of the other skills matter if a faster athlete can stop his passes because they efficiently close down space.

This is a sports lesson, but it's also a life lesson. Why? Because we live in a society that is constantly accelerating. It's an age of instant information, instant dissemination and instant gratification.

No matter what you choose to do, those doing it around you will be moving fast. Understanding how this evolution takes place on a soccer field, and how it also applies to you and your pursuit of excellence, translates to anything you choose to do in life.

Speed with a purpose
To be sure, speed in a vacuum isn't the goal. Playing fast can mean playing out of control, just as easily as it can mean dictating the pace of the game.

Fast movement must have a purpose. If a player is moving fast, without a purpose, the point is lost. Take for example a girl that we'll refer to as Victoria. She was one of the fastest players on one of Kendall's teams. She was not the most technically proficient, but she could run. Really, really run.

Often times, it looked like her body moved faster than her head. She would receive a pass, then turn and think about just one thing – scoring. More often than not, she would lose the ball for any number of reasons. Victoria's first touch was too big, she couldn't execute a particular move to navigate around a player, or she'd simply mishit the ball.

But one primary purpose – trying to score, every time she touched the ball – presents tremendous value. Combined with elite speed, that made her dangerous to opponents and valuable to her team.

Yes, by moving fast, she made mistakes. She made them often. But the speed she used to move the team downfield rattled defenders. As a result, the defenders also would make mistakes, creating opportunity for her teammates even when it didn't create opportunity directly for Victoria. Even speed with error was often better than slow with perfection.

The point of the story? Going fast, with a purpose, can lead to great things. Going fast, with mistakes, can still put you at an advantage.

So how do you get there?

Learning speed

Some athletes are naturally fast. Others are not. Interestingly, neither group is prepared to go fast with purpose. If you have mastered physical speed, you may need the purpose. If you're not naturally fast, you may have to learn both components. But, either way, you must learn.

Physical speed
Let's start here. Some are just born with natural speed. Others develop it. The elite do both.

Another of Kendall's teammates, who we'll call Cassie, was the fastest eleven-year-old girl many had ever seen. Rumor had it she held a national track record at the age of ten.

She regularly showed her speed during soccer games. Opposing players couldn't catch her in a dead sprint. That often led to great things – magnificent and improbable goals – as well as errors.

The assumption was that Cassie was just born with a unique gift. That may be true, but a conversation with those around her led to a different truth. Rumor had it that behind her house, Cassie had a steep hill. Her backyard was basically an uphill ramp. Since a young age, her father had been encouraging her to sprint up that hill almost daily. The only way to get faster is to sprint a lot. The only way to get faster than that… sprint uphill!

In other words, she had been building her physical speed for years and the results were apparent.

Some people are born fast, but everyone can train to improve running speed. Whether it's through participation at a speed and agility school or finding exercises on YouTube, there are many resources athletes can use to improve their speed.

Quickness works too
It's possible that even the most rigorous training will not make you an elite sprinter. That's ok. It's still possible to overcome that.

Playing fast isn't just for sprinters. Those with high-level *quickness* can play the game at world class levels as well. Playing fast doesn't always mean outrunning someone. It can mean leveraging intelligent positioning combined with sharp and rapid foot movement to outmaneuver opponents.

This may look different for different players. For some, it may be reactions – taking the right steps to the right places before opposing players. For others, quickness may come from body control – making more movements more quickly than other players, allowing one athlete to problem solve in tight spaces more efficiently.

As with sprinting, athletes can improve quickness through practice. It may focus on specific movements or training for general quickness. Either way, there's an opportunity to become better with sustained hard work.

Reading Coyle's book, *The Talent Code*, you come to understand that this type of functional quickness comes from deep practice – intentional repetition that is done with methodical precision, even slowly – which leads to muscle memory. When that has been achieved, an athlete can more easily make the same movements later with incredible speed.[12]

Quickness, in other words, can be developed slowly.

There's one additional consideration related to quickness versus speed. For those that learn to play fast through situational awareness, quickness is key. On a soccer field, it means you can pass more quickly, find openings more quickly, and execute on rapid decisions more quickly. In some cases, it's easier to play fast if you can actually run fast. But quickness also works and can often be more important. Find a way to improve the related physical attributes and you will play fast.

---

[12] Coyle, Daniel. *The Talent Code: Greatness Isn't Born. It's Grown. Here's How.* (New York: Bantam, 2009)

Situational awareness

How does thinking relate to playing fast? It's all about decision-making. Sit on the sideline of a soccer game long enough and you are bound to hear a coach say, "Know what you're doing with the ball before you get it." Coaches and players alike will tell you that the most important play is the next play. In other words, know the situation you are in so that you can make choices quickly. For example, know where your teammates are. Know where opponents are in relationship to your teammates. Choose to pass to the open player as a result. This certainly relates to our prior lesson about knowing your position (and another). That level of preparation helps you make better decisions. The better prepared your son is, the faster you can decide.

Improve upon that by choosing an option that will justify your son's pass, and also the next pass and the pass after that. See the game two or three moves ahead and his ability to play fast is related to seeing the future.

Similarly, by understanding both the game situation and the tactical situation, he can dictate the pace of play. Is his team trailing by a goal? Playing a more direct style of soccer – running directly at the defense to advance towards the goal more quickly – is advantageous. Improved situational awareness is the mental foundation for playing fast.

Preparation

Your son has trained and improved his physical speed. He's studied to improve a mental approach that will allow him to play fast. The last key element is preparation. Not the preparation required to improve the physical and mental skills. That's already been done.

Instead, we're talking about readiness to use those skills.

If he's put the work in to improve sprinting, he should prime his muscles to capitalize on that effort. Encourage him to stretch before a game.

If he's put in the work to ensure tactical awareness, he should prepare for his next opponent. Understand their tendencies and how that impacts what he may or may not see on the field. How will that change the decisions he'll face? He can make them faster because he's already considered the options.

Don't spend months training to play fast, then overlook the preparation required to realize the rewards of that hard work.

Fail fast
The other thing speed does is provide players and teams with the opportunity to fail fast, and then fix mistakes just as quickly.

If your daughter is moving slowly on the field, a mistake is magnified. If she's moving fast, she may lose the ball because her body is bordering on the edge of control. When she reaches that edge, and falls just a bit off, a turnover occurs. But once she's lost the ball, pursuing it just as quickly gives you a chance to disrupt the other team and potentially recover it. In other words, play fast on offense, but play faster on defense to reconcile an error.

Failing fast on the soccer field can often feel out of control, particularly for more conservative players. In reality, moving quickly means putting the other team on the defensive. If a fast player makes mistakes, then, her team should have the chance to fix them more easily.

Fast food
As a kid, it's easy to feel like you have all the time in the world. Then, as you get older, you realize how precious time is.

Kendall is often very decisive off the field, but not always. One of her favorite non-soccer activities is baking. In second grade, she entered a cupcake decorating contest, developed and executed the entire concept herself and finished in second place. Kendall found a way to design cupcakes to look like hamburgers, French fries and a milkshake. It was impressive and, for her, incredibly enjoyable.

Her interest in baking was apparent before that. But it burgeoned thereafter.

Even though she loves it, there are times when she would benefit from applying her *play fast* lessons to baking. It seems like an odd comparison, but when you outline her approach to baking and how she could accelerate it, the parallel becomes apparent.

On the rare day, when Kendall has neither soccer practice nor homework, she often decides she wants to bake. But then, she won't end up baking. Why? Because she moves slowly and never gets downfield. The progression looks a bit like this.

She decides she wants to bake (at the last minute).
She opens a cookbook to browse various recipes (without any specific direction).
That takes her about thirty minutes (of the two hours she has).
Then she chooses six recipes that appeal to her and spends five minutes narrowing it to three.
When she can't decide among the three recipes, she starts asking everyone what she should bake.
Ten minutes later, she finally chooses.
Then she starts locating the ingredients.
She doesn't have one or more of the ingredients, and gets frustrated, disappointed and sad.
We encourage her to just bake something else.
Begrudgingly, she agrees.
At this point, she has just enough free time left to complete the task at hand.
If she messes up, there's no opportunity to start over.

There's certainly not enough time to make multiple items.

Baking takes time. You can't accelerate the forty-five minutes required in the oven, just as you can't make the second half clock run faster to secure that early 1-0 lead and turn it into a win. But you can control speed around those set times.

Here, we can work the parallel in almost reverse order. To maximize her baking time, Kendall could prepare to bake faster. She can, when she has maybe just ten or fifteen free minutes, choose recipes she wants to bake. Then, she can list the needed ingredients. If she does these two things, then she eliminates time-consuming steps from that process.

Let's assume, however, that Kendall is still indecisive when the time comes. She has a few pre-selected recipes and all the ingredients, but she can't decide which delicious treat is more appealing. This is when playing fast, even if it leads to mistakes, is a preferable approach. Why?

With 120 minutes, Kendall actually has time to bake two items if she approaches it correctly. Her indecision comes from a fear of mistakes. She doesn't want to bake the *wrong thing* – which seems impossible when you're talking about delicious food. But, for Kendall, she wants to get it right. She wants to find the perfect balance of challenge, novelty and taste.

In spending time sorting through decision paralysis, she increases her odds of making a mistake. She ensures there is only enough time to make one item. If she's unhappy with it, there's no backup plan. If she's decisive and moves quickly, she could make two or three items in the same time used to bake one, so there's a better chance she will be happy with the outcome.

The same concept is true for many other life activities. In fact,

Kendall embraces speed in another of her hobbies.

Choose a book fast, read more, read faster
Kendall also loves to read, and yet she's decisive about choosing, starting and finishing books. It's an odd problem because, really, the same principles apply. There are so many books to read. What if she chooses the wrong one and doesn't like it. Then she's wasted time.

But she doesn't paralyze herself in that decision-making process. Instead, she is very comfortable choosing among many interesting titles, then consuming one with voracious speed. Kendall often realizes, quickly, that a book doesn't really interest her. So, she will stop and move on to another. Ask her at any moment, and she will tell you there's a pile of forty half-read books in the corner of her closet. More often than not, she will finish a book and then just move on to the second and third titles anyway. But, in all cases, she is prepared. She moves both with speed and quickness and understands that doing so let's her correct a "mistake" without wasted time.

What's the difference between the speed of choice and executing reading and baking? Product. When Kendall bakes, she is producing something. It's something in which she takes pride. She measures herself on the outcome. Whereas, with reading, she's a consumer. In other words, there's nothing at stake when she reads, but there is some level of personal value that she places in the act of baking. So, she contemplates it longer, more critically and with greater care.

The same can be said about approaching soccer. On the field, her choices have consequences – just like choosing a challenging recipe that might not turn out well. If she moves too quickly, she might play out of control and lose the ball. She will often choose to play more slowly, and conservatively. That has its own downside as well. In this case, comparing the soccer lesson and the life lesson reveal a critical insight. Ultimately, speed is about time and how it's used. Efficiency enhances your ability to use time. Playing fast, moving quickly, and failing (then fixing) early all produce more time, more repetitions and more opportunity to ultimately succeed.

Soccer moves fast. So, does life. If you're going to play either at the highest level, embrace speed and understand how to use it to your advantage.

Play Fast Actions

Everyone admires the naturally fast runners. But speed is about more than innate athletic ability. There are multiple factors that dictate whether you can play fast. There are also benefits that go well beyond beating an opponent. After those elements are understood, it's easier for you and your child to embrace the importance of playing fast as a life lesson. Here are some actions to reinforce this critical concept.

1. Redefine "fast" so that your child understands the expanded concept to include both physical and mental attributes. Only this more sophisticated understanding of "fast" can lead to a full appreciation of its benefits, and an awareness of how speed affects outcomes on the field.

2. Explore how different people achieve speed. Who is leveraging physical tools and who is leveraging mental tools? Are there clear examples of individuals who have mastered both?

3. Identify where your child is most naturally capable of playing fast. Accentuate those abilities and ensure they grow to become a clear strength. Then look at the area where speed is not a strength and talk about why. If your daughter runs fast but isn't situationally prepared, the first step towards improvement is building awareness.

4. Develop a plan to improve on "speed of play." Come up with a running routine and talk chalk. Take a balanced

KENT MALMROS

approach and revisit the chapter on making mistakes. Understanding that playing at speed will cause mistakes is critical to development.

5. Repeat steps one through four as it relates to math, art, cooking or music. Where can "playing fast" improve outcomes? How will failing fast improve overall growth?

Chapter Ten:
Want the Ball

October 19th

Dear Diary,
I love that Kendall is such a team player. It's one of my favorite things about her. While others want the personal glory of scoring, she has the maturity to understand that no one scores unless the team does its job. And that making a great pass is just as important as finishing.

It's pretty amazing that she understands that at such a young age. However, I keep trying to tell her that even to be unselfish ultimately, she has to be a little selfish at times. That's a harder concept to convey.

She's great at passing. But to be the outstanding passer and playmaker that she is, she still must want the ball. At times, she's having a bit more trouble understanding that. We try to tell her, but she genuinely associates being a good team player with being selfless. That's where we struggle.

We need to keep working on it, because wanting the ball in life will be important too. Even if you ultimately want to build your value in the accomplishments of others, you have to "want the ball" at certain times to get there.

Leaders — whether they are coaches, teachers, managers... anyone really — look for people to take control of a situation. Take responsibility. Organize a team. They look for someone to want the ball!

When you're young you think that means taking the final shot. It doesn't. You can still seek all the pressure situations without taking the final shot.

If we can explain that to Kendall and get her to really understand that, there's no limit to how great she can be. In soccer and in life.

Any ideas?

Sincerely,
Kent (aka, Soccer Dad)

Sometimes selfishness is selfless

In soccer, emphasis on playing the team game is critical. Great coaches put significant effort into unifying a group of people for the greater good. There's a reason they call it a team.

Watching Kendall's best coaches, a theme emerged consistently from within the team framework. Even with an emphasis on synchronizing the nine or eleven players on the field, and the entire roster over the course of a season and game, coaches still seek and reward individual excellence. Sometimes it's more dramatic than others. The cycle develops like this:

- *Players emphasize (entirely) individual attributes during a tryout with the intent of making a team.*
- *After they are selected, the practice sessions highlight team concepts almost exclusively.*
- *As games begin, players abandon 80% of the team concepts.*
- *Despite spending countless hours teaching "team," the coaches reward individuals.*

Maybe this is obvious to you. All team sports orchestrate individual achievement within a collective framework.

That's not the takeaway of this chapter, however. Because it's already understood that doing your job contributes to team success. The critical lesson can be seen when individual approaches are far more rewarded by the coach, even after he or she has dedicated hours to promoting team concepts. When game speed takes over, team concepts are harder to apply, and athletes revert to individualized actions.

And, yes, they are rewarded for it. Why? Well, there are a few reasons. First, coaches recognize that, no matter how much time is spent teaching team concepts, it takes years for athletes to embrace and execute them. If and until your child plays at a higher level (think, high school and beyond), coaches know they need standout individuals.

The second is about finding a form of leadership. Not vocal leadership, but rather leadership by example and performance. Even in the most team-oriented scenarios, great coaches seek players who are willing and interested in making those individualized plays when the time comes. They want someone to *want the ball.* They want someone that will take control of a situation and lead the team to victory.

It's not (necessarily) selfish
Some kids are just selfish. They want to score big goals, so they can be recognized. They want all the glory and all of the attention. As noted, bad coaches don't look too far past physical prowess and goal scoring. Great coaches will deter this.

It's also true, though, that five players can't simultaneously walk a ball into the goal. Sure, it may take four of the five to advance the ball down the field and ensure the team is in a position to score. But all five can't finish the play.

Ultimately, someone must take a shot on goal or the team doesn't score. That's how a team wins – by scoring. And that comes with pressure. A type of pressure that few players actually like or want. If no one wants to take the shot, are they all being selfless or ultimately a bit selfish?

In other words, it's not always selfish for a player to want to score. It's necessary to deliver the desired outcome. Coaches seek that player who wants to take the shot, particularly when it matters, because it's not easy. Yes, it should be done in the context of a team effort. But coaches need someone to *want* the ball.

When all else fails, or team concepts get you in front of the goal, but there's still a shot to be taken. The athlete that wants the ball is often the one that scores.

You can want the ball without scoring, too

We just completely blew up and contradicted Chapter Six in a few hundred words, right? *You said that not everyone scores and that's ok. This is a total contradiction!* Not exactly. Wanting to score is the most *obvious* example of wanting the ball. But not the only one.

There are other ways to "want the ball" without being the goal scorer. In fact, there are many ways to want the ball that dramatically impact the game and make a difference.

- *Goalkeepers can want to make a big save.*
- *Defenders can want to make a big tackle against an opponent on a breakaway (this is one of the highest-risk plays of all).*
- *Midfielders can want to carry the ball through the opposing team and make that perfectly placed final pass that builds up to the goal scoring opportunity.*
- *Wing players can want to take on a defender one-on-one and create the perfect crossing pass into the box so someone else can finish.*

These can and do represent situations where a player wants the ball. They differ in appearance, but they show desire to take command. The key is to run towards them, not away from them.

Ultimately, that's what the coach seeks – players that want to execute their role (and maybe a bit more) at the most important time of the game. When the pressure is on, and all eyes are watching.

Teamwork doesn't always get the job done when individual effort can. But an individual must want to make the effort. She must want the ball.

Kendall started to find this balance as her soccer career progressed.

151

Kendall played her under-twelve (U12) spring season as this book was being written. Her team at the time was talented in many facets of the game, but often lacked true offensive punch. At one point in her early career, Kendall had been a prolific goal-scorer. But during her under-ten and under-eleven years, she had shifted into more of a play-maker role, looking more often for the assist than the goal.

But this team needed more scoring ability, so she began playing more forward and seeking her own scoring opportunities regularly. Goals started occurring in bunches. Important and game-winning goals were part of the flurry. She had adjusted her game to recognize that becoming a scorer, again, was more selfless in this situation and would help her team win. As importantly, she knew how powerful it would be to provide the skill her team needed.

After scoring three game-winning goals in a four-game stretch, Kendall scored early in a critical late-season game. However, the team fell behind late in the second half. Her team was dominating the ball and creating chances, but they couldn't break through. With just a few minutes left, her team won a corner kick.

At younger ages, set pieces – the term for corner kicks and other free kicks – don't produce goals with any level of consistency. But they are still dangerous. Typically, the coach sends the girl with the most powerful legs to the corner to ensure the ball either gets near the goal or will be accidently and powerfully deflected into the net. With the powerful girls, the serve flew well over the box as often (and sometimes more often) than not.

Despite her rediscovered scoring ability, Kendall's most special skill remained vision and passing. She had a knack for seeing a spot, then making an accurate pass to find a teammate. Even on corners. Recognizing that they probably only had this chance left to tie the game, Kendall ran without hesitation to the corner and *wanted the ball* because she knew her service would have the highest probability of getting into the box without error. Because she would see a spot and deliver the ball there with accuracy. This would give her team a chance, at least.

She took three steps back, struck the ball and delivered an in-swinging serve that curved away from the outstretched feet of three different defenders, and found her teammate for a volley (meaning she hit the ball while it was still in the air, without letting it hit the ground) finish. The ball found the back of the net and tied the game.

For three weeks, Kendall had wanted the ball as a scorer. But in this case, she saw that wanting the ball again as a passer to enable someone else's goal was the most important role she could play for the team.

Why it matters
Highly functional teams require a subtle dance to take place between individual goals and group objectives. Athletes that want the ball understand how these two elements exist in harmony. If individual efforts can help a team achieve victory, both causes have been advanced. But it's hard to step into that role. Those that do, demonstrate three critical behaviors that improve the team performance:

- *Courage:* A championship soccer game is tied after ninety minutes and two overtime periods. It's time to determine a winner with penalty kicks. There's no rapid movement, no one-touch passing, no off-the-ball expertise. The ball is placed twelve yards away from the goalkeeper, then the whistle blows and you have one opportunity to put the ball into the back of the net. All eyes are on you. You can be the hero, but there's also a chance you will fail. That's terrifying. The desire to take on that challenge, in the face of failure, requires courage. There's no question that when you choose individual performance, there's as much downside as upside. Courage is the ingredient needed to overcome fear.

- *Confidence:* For some, courage is easier to muster. Maybe not everyone shares the same concern about consequences. One athlete may legitimately not care whether she misses that penalty kick at the end of the game. She would be happy with a good outcome but not defined by it. Even for an athlete who has courage, confidence is required to deliver results. Just being unafraid isn't wanting the ball. Being unafraid and having confidence is the form of "want" that makes individual effort a driver for team success.

- *Leadership:* Ultimately, great leaders must be willing to take the blame when their team fails and share the credit when the team succeeds. The same applies for an athlete that wants the ball. You can't take on the responsibility of the game winning shot without understanding and embracing all potential outcomes.

Teach it

The desire to win comes in all forms. Kids aren't always going to have the personality that drives them to take over a game at nine. Some may. Others may not. By eleven those traits may shift a bit. By fourteen, they may completely flip-flop.

Inherent personality traits may not change – that's a debate for a different book. But there's no question people can adjust how they leverage their talents to achieve success.

By observing sports practice, you see that great coaches don't necessarily accept a default mentality. They explain the need to want the ball and then reward kids that embrace it. Creating a safe place where mistakes are condoned, where they are rewarded instead of punished, is critical to establishing such a culture.

If you want athletes to want the ball, you need to create a safe environment for them to take risks.

In some countries, this sense of experimentation is cultivated at the youth level by playing competitive games without keeping score – until players reach their teens. Imagine what could be learned by taking individual risks in a team environment if we didn't keep score? More young athletes would demonstrate courage, confidence and leadership. In other environments, it's important to find ways to make it safe to experiment, so that the best behaviors can be taught by parents and coaches, then embraced by kids.

A cautionary tale

We've walked through this chapter assuming most kids don't want the ball – that they shy away from the spotlight. But what happens when a child wants the ball too much. On the field or off the field?

This is an interesting counterpoint to the core lesson. Let's start with the soccer field. As we mentioned earlier, coaches tend to reward kids that show an inclination to want the ball. Even if they want it too much.

As a parent, your job is to both encourage your daughter to simultaneously maintain and curtail the approach. Why? Because there's a fine line between selfish play for selfless ends, and selfish play that's detrimental to the team outcome.

If your daughter only focuses on scoring, how often is she ignoring the easy pass to the open player that could result in more goals for the team? How often is her aggression, driven by a desire to score, leading to turnovers? How often does she make the risky play when the safe play is more obvious and helpful?

It's great that she wants the ball. It's great that your daughter can more easily embrace the pressure and embody the courage required

155

to help the team at tough moments. You want to make sure she retains that, even as you encourage her to think more about the overall good of the group.

The best way to accomplish this comes by emphasizing other ways to lead, without the glory of a goal. Outline the great moments that come from an exceptional pass or defensive play. Celebrate the non-scoring assertiveness of other teammates, and make sure to do so with vigor for your daughter as well.

Wanting the ball too much is both a blessing and a curse, but it requires the same consideration from parents to balance the benefits with your children.

Who's going to speak?
Public speaking is often regarded as one of the most terrifying acts. You walk up to a podium or onto a stage, prepared to deliver some type of talk in front of one, ten or five hundred people. The degree of anxiety may vary, but it's hard for almost everyone. There are ways to overcome the fear, but it takes time and practice. Still, even when you employ mechanisms to make public speaking easier, fear creeps up.

Imagine you're about to step onstage. Preparation was fantastic. Rehearsals were excellent. Yet, sweat has developed in your palms, dryness is creeping up your throat and into the back of your mouth, and vision seems blurry. The only thing preventing you from stepping back off stage is a desire to fulfill your objective. For whatever reason, you want the ball.

Most people have experienced these sensations. You've worked as part of a group, maybe on a research project. But when the time comes to present your findings, someone needs to stand in front of a room and deliver the right message. Despite the fear of public speaking, it's necessary to step into the spotlight to complete the objective. Your young athlete understands these types of situations as well – when team and individual excellence intersect for the benefit of the whole.

In the classroom, group projects create this scenario. Your son is paired with four other students to research Ancient Greece. The team is tasked with creating various deliverables based on their research. Maybe they need to create a poster or diorama. Then, they are required to make a presentation.

At a very young age, students are asked to face that fear of public speaking. A highly functional team with well-defined roles and easy information exchange suddenly becomes challenged. Who is going to take on the lead role in the presentation. Who wants the ball?

In this instance, at least one student needs to demonstrate courage, confidence and leadership. Who is going to embody these characteristics when they are critical to the team's outcome?

If no one speaks (wants the ball) the team's grade will suffer (lose the game). When teachers consider individual grades, they are looking for the students willing to show the courage, confidence and leadership to put their group's work on display. Even if the outcome (the speech) is imperfect, those students are likely to be rewarded for their efforts.

Want the ball if you aspire to lead. Make no mistake, this lesson will last well into adulthood. Every group needs someone that wants the ball.

On a soccer field, wanting the ball is about initiative. It's a leadership quality. It's a desire to show people that fear inhibits effort, and a lack of effort derails the desired outcome.

Stephanie can't dance

We explored the dynamics of a dance solo in an earlier chapter. In that case, we compared it to scoring goals. Not everyone can score and not everyone can get a solo.

But, just as we've discussed how the selfless soccer player can still *want the ball* the right way, so to can the selfless dancer.

At one of Hayden's recent recitals, such a situation arose. A girl in her class, Stephanie, became ill days before the year-end recital. She was a good dancer, and prominent in the choreography. She was sick enough – diagnosed with pneumonia – that she was unable to dance in the season's final show.

Often, when someone is absent from a dance, the rest of the choreography remains the same.

But what happens when a dancer like Stephanie has a solo that needs to be performed? Or a space that needs to be filled on stage to ensure the dance is smooth. At that point, no one wants the solo, because they haven't learned or practiced it. They haven't spent time to ensure they can be their personal best.

But the routine will suffer more if no one steps up. The company needs a dancer to be selfish for the sake of the other dancers. Someone needs to take a risk, and potentially claim the glory, for the recital to work for everyone.

Who wants the ball in those situations?

Building a winning culture often comes down to such scenarios. Identifying, embracing and rewarding those individuals. Learn it on the soccer field and carry it with you throughout life.

Want the Ball Actions

As a coach or parent, we often assume, erroneously, that kids are just born with the desire to "want the ball" or not. Sure, some kids are more intrinsically capable of embracing this role. But, these qualities can be cultivated in young athletes. Give your athlete various scenarios to consider and explore and watch them want the ball more as time goes on.

1. Contextualize the importance of wanting the ball for the right reasons. If your child is more prone to be a team player, it may be hard for her to break free of selfless habits. Praise that mentality but be sure to explain when "selfishness" is also better for the team. Appeal to selfless behavior to bring out individuality.

2. Study specific actions in your athlete's sport that exemplify individual excellence, in the right context. On a soccer field, it's not dribbling fifty yards for no reason, ignoring open teammates the whole way, just to lose the ball at the end of your run. It is taking a difficult shot, when your team is down by a goal and it's the best opportunity you've had to score. These situations may be out of character, but they can generate positive outcomes for the team.

3. Explain the extended benefits of maximizing individual opportunities. Talk about how showing courage and confidence can demonstrate leadership. Explore how leadership qualities attained this way ultimately improve the overall team dynamic.

4. Encourage your young athlete to embrace these opportunities, even in the face of "failure," and explain how the upside is far greater than the downside. Fall back on applauding and praising drive and passion, not outcomes.

Revisit fun and talk about how enjoyable these competitive situations can be.

5. Regularly examine where wanting the ball is appropriate in other life scenarios – from school to theater to social situations and beyond. What are the equivalent actions of taking a shot late in the game when your team is behind? How do these situations help your child's "team" of choice?

Chapter Eleven:
Talk. Then Talk More!

October 25th

Dear Diary,

I think young athletes are embarrassed to talk on the field. That's the only explanation for it, because coaches beg them to do it, and they just won't. Coaches will teach them technical skills and tactical awareness. They will beg them to shoot a certain way, or run a certain way, they assume the kids will do it.

But when a coach asks them to communicate, they just won't. That's not exactly true. They talk a little, but just a little. They speak softly, and intermittently. Meanwhile, coaches are begging them to bark out helpful information to teammates, so they can evade a defender or move in the right direction. Anything to make the team function well together.

It has to be about identity. Kids just don't have a strong enough sense of self to feel confident that their voice matters. So, they remain quiet. As they get older it changes – fourteen-year old soccer teams are ten-times louder than twelve-year old teams! But why can't they learn that lesson earlier and more intentionally? Communication is so important in life. If there's a communication gap, giving a bit more than everyone else can make you stand out. It also helps the team so much.

I need to keep encouraging Kendall to talk. I know she has it in her. I want to encourage her to really talk, then talk some more.

Sincerely,
Kent (aka, Soccer Dad)

Talking takes time, for some reason

Standing on the sidelines for hours of soccer practice, there's one dramatic difference you will notice between an eleven-year old girls' team, and a fourteen-year old girls' team. Yes, clearly, they are different physically. The size, strength and aggressiveness reflect that. But on a relative basis, you can watch equally skilled and athletic teams three-years apart and not be struck by a massive discrepancy in technical or tactical capabilities.

Those characteristics grow in a relatively linear fashion. But communication changes on an exponential curve.

It gets loud

What strikes you most is the volume. Not the volume of the fans. Not the volume of the coaches. The volume of the players' voices.

It's often shocking. Younger girls' teams are relatively quiet. Regardless of how much their coaches encourage a team to talk, they genuinely struggle with it. Even when they talk, they don't scream and yell. They don't do it on every touch. They don't make it a core part of the game as they play.

Speak with various coaches about this phenomenon and they will tell you it's commonplace. The magic age range appears to be around twelve. That's when girls start becoming more naturally vocal and by thirteen, it just becomes a naturally evolving part of the routine. Before that, no matter how much a coach incorporates communication into their training routine, it just doesn't stick. At least not with the ubiquity you'll notice as girls get older.

It changes the game, too. Entirely.

As team sports progress, communication must as well. So that evolution immediately makes teams better. They can play more cohesively by supporting one another. For example, players may give their teammates situational information. In doing so, they begin to operate more efficiently.

In soccer, there are several standard ways you communicate.

- *Man-on* typically means you have a defender behind you.
- *Turn* is a way to tell a player with the ball they should rotate (probably 180 degrees) because there is open space behind her.
- *No turn* is a way to let a defender know you think the player with ball is likely to turn quickly to either dribble past you, or shoot, and that they should be ready to stop them.
- *Here* is simply a way to let someone know you think you are open and want the ball.

Short bursts of communication become the currency that makes your team a unified economy of transactions. It's imperative for a team to communicate actively and often if they want to excel.
This generalized, and more commonplace communication makes a major difference. But, there's more.

Great teams get specific
Great teams take it to another level. Their communication becomes more frequent, more precise and more sophisticated. Watch the most communicative teams and their coaches. You notice a deliberate effort to train verbal cues into practices. They encourage their players to talk, then talk, then talk more. Every time they are on the ball, they are talking. When players are off the ball, they are talking. In other words, they are always talking.

What you see is a group of eleven players constantly communicating in short bursts of targeted information that helps them act as one. They are a group of individuals willing to support each other in every way possible to achieve a common goal.

Whereas a team using basic communication will say *man on* to help a teammate know when a defender is approaching them, the evolved team does much more. They tell that same player *man on* three or four times, loudly and assertively. They will also deliver the location. *Man on, left shoulder.* Most likely, they will give precise guidance on the time they arrive. *Man on, left shoulder, two yards.*

Consider the magnitude of this addition and its impact. The player now has enough data to make several critical decisions. Once she receives the ball, she knows in which direction it's safest to move. She understands she may be able to take a first touch to their right to avoid the defender to her left. She also has a sense for which direction may be the most open for a pass to a teammate.

Those decisions may dictate the team's ability to find open space, setup a goal, and then score.

Great listening empowers talking
There's another side of talking that's been implied to this point. If eleven members of a team are talking, it's only effective if they are also listening to each other.

This chapter is more specifically about building speaking behaviors. So, we won't delve too far into the other side of the equation. But make sure to explore this with your child. If the team is talking to your child, he needs to listen.

The better he listens, the more effective his teammates' communication will be. Moreover, the better he is as a listener, the better he will become as a talker. Why? Because he'll hear what language his teammates use, then develop a shared vernacular.

Eleven players on the field shout short communications to help each other solve problems – maneuver past a defender, make the safest pass, find open space and more. Communication itself is a living, breathing organism that changes shape and stature as the game goes on. It only works when the players are both talking and listening. As we've suggested, there's a direct correlation between the health and vibrancy of that organism and the success of the team. Great communication leads to great results.

The normality of communication

How does this life lesson apply off the soccer field? Travel down the hall to the shared bathroom of two tween girls in the morning. As they get ready for school, elbows bump at the sink. They get in each other's way when they could easily avoid each other. They simply aren't talking.

They move in the same space, battling for the same tools, working on similar timelines. Their goals are simultaneously different and exactly the same – get dressed, eat breakfast, pack bags, brush teeth and get out the door. They most definitely aren't competing because they are getting on different buses, at different times, taking them to different schools.

But, they wake up at roughly the same time. They started moving through their routines at the same time. So, at some point, they begin to act like they are competing. The build-up and timing of the conflict is somewhat predictable.

At first, it starts with wanting to use the toothpaste at the same time. Then they reach for the same brush. Eventually, they look for different clothes in the same laundry basket. Each real-time need leads them separately to the same place, at the same time. Quietly. Eventually, their silent conflict erupts into a screaming match. They fail to communicate, and that failure led to an outright blow-up.

The same types of short-burst communication that Kendall uses (or should use) on the soccer field can be leveraged in the bathroom. Just as trainers encourage her teammates to help each other navigate tight spaces, so too can we encourage our kids to navigate the house with minimal but consistent information. Imagine the moment they both go into the bathroom. The entire outburst above can be negotiated if the girls just talk, and then talk more.

When they reach for the toothpaste at the same time, Kendall could offer that she plans to brush her teeth now because it's the last thing she needs to do before walking out the door to catch her bus – which arrives an hour earlier than Hayden's.

When they reach for the same brush, Hayden can mention that she knows Kendall's brush is on the counter in the next room. And that she needs a specific hair brush because it better works out the knots in her hair.

As far as the laundry basket is concerned, whomever gets there first can ask the other what clothes she is looking for, and then offer to retrieve them on her behalf.

Communication would allow them to help each other and navigate a tight situation.

An example from mom or dad's life
Communication matters in school. We've used many school room examples to emphasis life lessons. There are also situations in corporate boardrooms that equally reflect this principle learned on the soccer field. It's great to use such examples with your children so they see the lasting value of lessons learned on the soccer field.

One such example might look like this. A customer support representative for a software company, let's call her Patty, received a call from a customer. They found a bug in the software that has completely halted their business. Patty perfectly executed her job by listening to the customer, asking clarifying questions, understanding and documenting the problem.

If her next step was to notify her manager, it would be like a midfielder on a soccer team stopping in the midfield and staring at her coach. Things would keep moving around her and most likely she would lose the ball and force herself into a reactive position.

But Patty took a different approach – the rapid communication approach. She recognized the challenge at hand and once it was clear that the bug was real, she went to work.

While still on the phone, in between taking notes, she messaged her customer support peers and suggested they check on other inbound calls or emails. She provided a short description of the issue and asked them to see if others are having the same problem.

As her peers worked on it, she completed the call ensuring she had contact information, so she could update the customer.

Based on her experience, Patty knew that this issue was not related to user error. It was a bug in the platform that has been exposed. As a result, her next move was to visit the development team.

She didn't seek out the *manager* of the development team. Instead, Patty found senior developers and architects. People that knew and understood the code. She described the issue, conveying every collected detail to them, and then left them to start their own root cause analysis. The development team also gave Patty some ideas of what may have been going on, so she could provide feedback to the customer if necessary.

The next conversation was with management, right? Not even close.

Patty walked over to the account team. In this company, someone was responsible for managing the day-to-day relationship with customers. Specifically, when custom work was completed. Think of the role like as someone that guides projects to successful completion, then builds a personal relationship to become a partner. Because they were essentially the face of the company to the client, Patty wanted to both make sure the lead account manager *knew* about the problem. Patty also wanted them to start working in the background to get more details on what led to the issue. That team gave Patty an idea of which other stakeholders may be involved behind the scenes.

Next, it was time to tell the sales team. Patty knew there was a good chance that her colleagues were actively trying to sell new products to the customer. She wanted to ensure they were prepared. *The team's striker comes off the field for a substitution and immediately tells her incoming teammate where she sees a weakness in the opposition defense.*

Then, finally, Patty told management what was going. In doing so, she could inform them of all steps she had taken towards resolution.

The issue got resolved. Quickly, without any additional major challenges. Patty's ability to communicate with her colleagues as if she was a midfielder made all the difference. Talk, then talk some more, in any team scenario.

Just as great soccer coaches train their team to talk, talk more, and talk at the right levels – those that execute the work and need to solve problems in real-time – great siblings at home and great managers at the office, ensure their teams are built to do the same.

Talk. Then Talk More! Actions
Coaches develop drills that require communication and you can do the same in everyday life. This will reinforce those key behaviors at home with your young athlete. These behaviors, exhibited daily, can get your team working like a fluid and dynamic soccer team. You're also using them off the field. Short bursts of communication geared towards solving problems will become a valuable tool for your child.

1. Discuss in detail why on-field communication is important. Make sure your child knows that it's ok to be the one to talk, even when others aren't. Emphasizing the value of communication – and specifically asking your child to consider how gaining information helps them – will reinforce why it is such a critical asset.

2. Encourage your child to talk to her teammates off the field as well. The more she does, the more natural it will feel to talk while playing. This is true in other facets of life. If you communicate in low-stakes scenarios, you'll be comfortable doing so in high-stakes scenarios as well.

3. Emphasize the power of listening. This will help you build a vocabulary around chosen areas of interest. Know the right terms to use on a soccer field. Likewise, learn terminology to use around the classroom, the house, the library or anywhere else you interact with others who can impact your performance.

4. Talk about talking. That's right, when you sense that communication can help a group to function well, explore better ways to execute. Speak with your child and encourage him to talk to their teammates about the importance of communication.

5. Model this at home. Review family activities and make sure communication is embedded in them. Whether it's making dinner or cleaning the living room, modeling the usefulness of talking and listening is important to modelling it in behavior.

Part Three:
Coming off the Field

(Focus on Outcomes and Interpretation)

Chapter Twelve:
Know Your Bias

October 29th

Dear Diary,
Kendall walks on water. So does Hayden. After all, they are my daughters. And that's the way it should be.

But, as one of Kendall's coaches once told me, that makes you look at your daughter's ability through rose-colored glasses. He was right. You never see your own child's talent with complete objectivity.

Kendall's accomplishments do speak for themselves, though. And that's the thing I tend to focus on when we discuss her performance on the soccer field — results and productivity. It's the only way to discuss something untainted by emotion.

While I'm finding the rose-colored glasses may never become completely clear, it's very easy to help Kendall develop just by observing. By knowing my bias and combatting it with data-driven discussions. I keep track of her playing time. Not to complain (or boast), but rather as a data point.

If she played less than other players, it's just data and a way to ask, "Why do you think other people played more? What did the coach see that kept them on the field?"

I can keep track of when she scores a goal, or notches an assist or steal. Conversely, I also keep track of when she loses the ball or has a pass intercepted. More data!

Using data, I don't have to worry about being a partial observer. I just present impartial facts to Kendall and we talk about what they mean to her, her coach and her teammates. If I do it the right way, it can be helpful.

Really, that is how she should go through life. Acquiring and interpreting data while filtering through less relevant noise surrounding a situation. Another life lesson to be learned through soccer.

Sincerely,
Kent (aka, Soccer Dad)

Persistent bias

Every parent has an inflated opinion of their child's talent. Ok, maybe not every parent, but the majority. It's parental pride and it makes good sense. Parents both want the best for their children and err on the side of encouragement through positive reinforcement.

What does it look like? Pretty simple, really. You tell your child they are talented, capable and ready to become a star. Maybe not always a star, but if they are on the bench, you probably tell them they should be starting. You tell them they are good! Certainly, better than the coach or anyone else may think they are because you want them to be confident. You want them to believe.

It's not going anywhere

Even if you recognize your bias, it's virtually impossible to filter it out of your approach. As parents, we're just wired this way.

To be sure, you'll have moments of clarity. Your daughter is on the field, ready to take over the game by scoring an amazing goal in the last five minutes. You've seen the future and it's going to happen – all she needed was the chance!

But instead, reality plays out a bit differently. Your daughter enters the game and her first touch is a poor one. She loses the ball. Then, she struggles to get past her defender and is largely ineffective for her stint on the field. The outcome registers, and momentarily you realize maybe she isn't quite the budding superstar you believed.

A few minutes later, your bias returns. You focus on whatever positives existed and begin to justify the poor showing. Maybe it was the conditions. Or that your daughter couldn't get into a rhythm. Maybe she didn't mesh well with the other girls on the field. That moment of objectivity disappears, and the biased parent re-appears. It probably begins to revise history, possibly even in making excuses. Either way, that moment of clarity fades away.

Recognize, own and work around it

If nothing else, recognize that you had such a moment of clarity. Hold onto it, knowing that it is likely impossible to become fully objective. In fact, hold onto it knowing that you don't even want to become completely objective. Instead, you will need to shift your approach and that's what this chapter is about.

It can be as harmful as helpful

The thing about parenting with bias is that it can be both good and bad.

Let's start with the good. As a parent, your primary objective should be to instill confidence in your child. The confidence to try. The confidence to fail. The confidence to dust yourself off after that failure, improve and try again. The confidence that they will be loved no matter what they do or don't do on a soccer field.

To be sure, sports is a playground for failure. And constant encouragement and reinforcement can keep your child believing and motivated in the face of that failure.

There is a right way to encourage your child. Encouragement should largely focus on a growth mindset instead of a fixed mindset. There's an increasing amount of literature that decries praise based only on outcomes. Even though it seems like positive reinforcement, it can have reverse effects. The recipient of that feedback may start to think that a less perfect outcome will lead to negative feedback. That can discourage risk-taking or promote a fear of failure. It can discourage creativity. Yes, failure is and should be a positive experience. The outcome of a failed experience is just data acquired through trial and error to be used on the path to improvement.

As parents, you know that accomplishment-based kudos will creep into your communications. We are naturally happy when our children achieve the outcomes they desire. We internalize and begin to own those desires ourselves. The praise looks like this. *What a great pass. The goal was outstanding. You're so fast! You're definitely the best player on the field.*

The unaware biased parent delivers that praise and doesn't think twice about it. However, the objective parent who recognizes their role takes a different approach by rewarding the effort. *I'm so proud of your effort. You work so hard. Your hard work showed today when you scored that goal.*

Expectation invasion

When expectations sneak into the equation, things change. Parents begin to anticipate results and it becomes impossible for them to praise anything else. The bias that was or could have been encouragement turns into something closer to a vision that you create for your child. This is when it turns bad. It can be harmful in three key ways.

1. *Misguidance.* When those moments of clarity completely evaporate, you may start to give your child feedback that's not grounded in a growth mindset. Instead of focusing on a balanced set of data – what was done well, what could be better – conversations about your child's performance begin to focus *only* on their achievements or talent.

   There is little-to-no objective feedback about where improvements need to take place. There is little-to-no encouragement about improvement and hard work as an end goal. The discussions begin to center on comparisons to other players. This is dangerous because the impartiality has changed from confidence-building to deceiving.

2. *Elevated expectations.* The next step, then, is disappointment. Parents that are misguided about their child's talent develop

expectations. *"My daughter is (or should be) the star of this team. She should be scoring goals in every single game."*

Walk around any soccer field in the United States, during autumn, and you can be sure that an alarming number of parents think like this. Even if just ten percent of parents do, with over three million kids playing soccer every year, that's 300,000 athletes whose parents believe they are on the verge of being discovered because of their transcendent talent. When you consider that a single generational talent, someone that transcends the standards set before, comes along every ten years or so, that's a huge number of parents creating unreasonable expectations.

Because of their expectations, they become constantly disappointed. They take their disappointment out on their kids for no good reason. In turn, sports are no longer fun and ultimately the child may quit, resent their parents or both.

3. *Unbalanced interpretation.* Disappointment can come from another place as well. Elevated expectations typically drive negativity when a child fails to feature or star. But, after that happens, parental vision also loses clarity.

When parents are frustrated by their child's performance, they may magnify the child's mistakes. No matter what the child does, the parents see errors. They think their child is the worst player on the field, regardless of their actual performance. They forget that other kids make mistakes too.

If you're a parent and you reach this point, it's time to re-evaluate. You're doing more damage than good. Possibly even being destructive. You are likely crushing confidence, giving bad advice and discouraging the mistakes your child should be embracing.

Bias may seem like positivity. But it prevents you from providing your child with the data required to maximize her experience playing sports. There's no question that you want to encourage your child. Rewards and recognition are a big part of that. You need to reward the right things.

Focus on efforts, not outcomes

That means that, as hard as it may be, you can't solely acknowledge the goal scoring, or the big save. Ensure the correlation is made between what happens on the field, and what has been done leading up to those moments. That means focusing on the efforts, not just the outcomes.

Yes, of course there is a correlation. You need to discuss what has happened on the field in order to connect something to effort – the results, right!? But, that's really the critical factor is underscoring the cause of (passion and) drive and the results associated with that drive.

Now, when you start assessing the outcomes to get back to the value of hard work, it's easy to go sideways. But, that doesn't have to happen.

Focus on data, not opinion

The easiest way to focus on the right association of outcomes is by relying on observation-derived data. Don't editorialize. Just cite facts.

What exactly does that mean? It means if you're trying to reward effort based on outcome. For example, talk about how shooting 100 times, three extra days over the past two weeks contributed to your son's goal scoring efforts. Conversely, if your son didn't play as much as he wanted, emphasize he could have used more of his time to improve.

Either way, the data can help you get to that point. There are so many levels of understanding that parents need to achieve. Maybe you think your kid is the best player on the team. But the data suggests otherwise.

On the negative side...
- He played less than half the game
- When he received the ball, he lost it easily
- He was outrun by his opponents

On the positive side…

- He started
- When he had the ball, he registered multiple shots on goal
- He won multiple tackles and earned the ball for his team

None of these are about how you perceived him to play. They are what you *saw* occur in the game. They are observations based on actions. They are devoid of editorial comment.

Playing less than half the game, particularly when four others played the entire game, might not support him being the team's best player. That's one conclusion that can be drawn from the data. It's his conclusion to draw, but you can point him to the evidence.

Once he does, there's an opening to have a conversation. He has come to the challenging conclusion that his capabilities are not where he wants them to be.

This gives you a platform to explore effort – either how it led to the desired outcome, or how there is opportunity for more or different efforts that could lead to different outcomes. Has he put in enough

science, where results are based on objective outcomes. In English or language arts, however, you immediately find yourself dealing in shades of gray.

You daughter has spent weeks working on a research paper involving literary criticism of a well-known novel. She's been diligent, without a hint of procrastination. At each step of the project, your daughter has sought feedback from her teachers, who made recommended and requisite changes alike.

The project has been challenging and full of growth opportunities, much like training or practice during a soccer season. Through the draft process, she has handled critical feedback with aplomb. It hasn't dissuaded her. In fact, she continues to take a few risks with her writing, eager to make any corrections provided. It's been a struggle, but she's confident the effort was worthwhile.

Those efforts have all led to the equivalent of gameday – the final essay to be handed in for a whopping thirty percent of her marking period grade. She has put in the work and hands in the paper.

Weeks go by, and a grade is finally returned. To her surprise, the red pen at the top of her paper reveals a "C" and not the "A" she had expected.

Your daughter is immediately distraught. Her months of hard work feel like a waste and the outcome has left her completely deflated. *Why bother doing the work,* she thinks, *if this is going to be the outcome.*

As a parent, you feel for your child. You want what is best for her. But as a biased parent, you begin to focus on the outcomes relative to expectations. Maybe, just as we explored on the soccer field, you lean towards the side of misguidance. The teacher must hate your daughter, you say. Focus turns to other kids and their grades. You tear them down to try and make her feel better. Meanwhile, your child feels worthless, regardless of her many accomplishments outside of that class.

Suppress the commentary

Sure, let your daughter vent. She needs to and that's what you're there for. When that's said and done, fight the urge to attack everyone else for her shortcomings. It's not productive and it lets your bias rear its ugly head.

Remember the lessons in Chapter Three: Make Mistakes. It's not about outcomes. A focus solely on outcomes will be detrimental to the long-term life lessons that both sports and school should be teaching your child.

You daughter did the research.
She wrote the outline.
She wrote the rough draft.
She sought feedback from her teacher at every step.
She committed to the final product and put the time in.

The grade was disappointing to be sure. Twenty years from now, that's what she's likely to remember. But it won't matter because she will be using the tools developed during that process – research, outlining, drafting, feedback, etc. – to deliver on a project plan, proposal, grant application or something else. The grade will be forgotten. The skills she developed along the way will persist.

In the moment, however, you should deal with her reaction to the grade. It's time to turn to data and inquiry. Yes, ask what her classmates got, but not so you can chastise their capabilities relative to hers. Instead so you can use inquiry to uncover opportunities for growth.

So, Anna got an "A" on her paper. Did she start sooner? Did she do more research? Did she work with the teacher more?

The answers may not immediately uncover the growth opportunity. But suppress the parental bias that believes your daughter is automatically an "A" student. It will force you to fact-broker and guide your daughter through introspection. She will have to see the data and make her own assessment.

The job market

If your child is a teenager, he may also be entering the workforce for the first time. Here is another scenario where being an objective observer will serve both you and your child well.

Maybe your son wants to work at the local eatery. Again, don't let partiality play a role in your preparation and subsequent analysis of the interview process. Collect and disseminate data, then use inquiry to help him reach the goal.

Yes, you think he would be an outstanding bus boy at the popular local eatery around the corner. But observe and document. What type of kid does the establishment typically hire? Are they dressed a certain way? Does the restaurant have a particular approach to customer service? Has your son effectively figured out how he fits into that?

Ask your son about these concepts as he prepares for his interview. Talk about the bias he is trying to overcome in that situation – his and other people's.

His excellence may well get him the job. But, a self-aware parent will suppress those feelings and figure out how to objectively help him ensure the best possible outcome.

Objective observation, fact-brokering and reflection will guide you with greater clarity than emotion. As a parent, you can model this behavior for your child. The faster they learn how to filter out bias, theirs and yours, the easier the journey will become easier.

Know Your Bias Actions

Understanding the role of bias, and then figuring out how to suppress it for some level of objectivity, is a prime example. The following actions will help you embrace this concept.

1. Recognize, as a parent, when you're the most biased. Partiality creeps into the equation often, and it will happen to you. Note your challenges the way that most makes sense for you. If that means writing it down, take that step.

2. Talk to your child about where bias – yours and theirs – can creep in, and why it's valuable to rely on fact and objectivity. The more your child knows about the bias you are trying to overcome, to help him improve, the more you can be aligned towards an outcome.

3. Become the best possible objective observer and encourage your child to do the same. This is the only way you can truly collect helpful data. As parents of youth athletes, we tend have tunnel-vision, and watch only the exploits of our children. Start watching other athletes so you can objectively present your child with data-driven findings of his performance versus others.

4. Leverage inquiry to help your child correlate actions to outcomes. They are on the inside – attending practice every day and listening to a coach's feedback. Your opinion is just that, your opinion. So, when they ask for it, push them to look inward and truly scrutinize the situation from all angles.

5. Ask your child to give you the same type of objective information as you navigate your life. Having them suppress their own bias (yes, kids are biased about their parents as well) to collect data and help you correlate actions to

outcomes will make them better at seeing their own opportunities for growth.

Chapter Thirteen:
Good Coaches, Bad Coaches

October 29th

Dear Diary,
It would be nice for Kendall to have a great coach every year. But there are two problems with thinking like that. First, everyone has a different opinion about the same coach. Kendall may love someone that another girl dislikes.

The second problem is that when you worry about the coach, you stop focusing on the things you can control such as fun, drive and improvement. Yes, of course coaches are a factor in helping you improve. But, ultimately you can't control your coach. You can only control how hard you work to achieve your goals.

This conversation sounds a lot like those we've had regarding teachers or friends. No matter what you do in life, people are a big part of the journey. And you come across a lot of people. If you let them impact your desire to reach a certain outcome, they will. If you focus on what you can control – your attitude, effort and persistence – the challenging individuals become bumps in the road. It's easy to say and hard to do.

That's what I want to focus on talking to Kendall about. She will have good coaches, she will have bad coaches. She can't control that. But she can control how she reacts and responds to them. If she can figure that out through soccer, she'll be better off than I was early in life.

Sincerely,
Kent (aka, Soccer Dad)

People can kill passion

Business magazines and websites often publish features on the importance of passion in entrepreneurs. Find what you love and do it well. Do it better than others. The money will follow!

That's an oversimplification of the process, to be sure. But there's a reason business advice emphasizes passion – because success requires hard work, and hard work is often difficult and exhausting. If you're not passionate, you may give up. Enjoying the craft on which you're focused makes it easier to sustain effort over a long period of time.

Whether it's business or sports, there are times when you just don't feel like getting out of bed and jumping into the grind. Loving the art of the deal, or the art of a scoring goals, makes the sweat a bit more tolerable. That's why there's so much focus on passion as a catalyst for long-term pursuits. Passion allows you to be self-motivated and driven by an internal pursuit. It's a guiding principle that also helps you overcome additional external challenges.

One of those external challenges comes in the form of coaches. A good coach isn't a challenge. In fact, a good coach can be the catalyst towards the passionate pursuit of greatness. But a bad coach – regardless of how you define it – can be debilitating, often to the point of destroying your child's love of any game. A bad coach is characterized by several things. Maybe they are just mean. Or negative. Uneducated and incapable of improving your child's skills. Volatile. Emotionally abusive. There are so many characteristics that can be associated with a bad coach.

Bad coaches are not just demanding. Coaches are not bad because your child doesn't play. Those are normal challenges of the coach-athlete dynamic. Be very careful to differentiate between a tough coach and a bad coach.

Everyone has a slightly different definition and we'll leave it to you to come up with your own.

Regardless, coaches are external factors that impact internal beliefs. It seems unfair for someone – often a stranger – to have this strong an impact on a young life. But, that's a hard reality that playing youth athletics can teach. The life lesson, then, is understanding how to deal with it.

Coaches come in all shapes and forms

Walk around a soccer field on a fall weekend and you'll be struck by, yes, the insane parents. But also, by the wide array of coaching styles you encounter. For good reason. Coaches range from willing parents who have never played a sport to highly trained paid professionals that do nothing else but coach. Experience suggests that neither extreme is ideal, but it's the current reality. With the demand for youth sports at an all-time high, there simply aren't enough coaches available to standardize an approach.

The correlation between coaching style and quality isn't obvious either. The clueless parent might be a great coach for your son. The paid professional could cause high levels of anxiety. It's not always what you'd expect.

Variance for all

If your child never plays more than intramural sports, you're likely to see the parent-coach archetype. And maybe nothing more. If you advance to travel sports or beyond, playing with "elite" clubs that travel great distances, you'll get exposure to the paid coaches of the world.

Here's the reality: no matter the type, you'll have good coaches and bad coaches. It's bound to happen if you play sports long enough.

Here's the second reality: there's nothing you can do about it.

Good coaches are among life's great blessings. They connect with your child and bring out the best in her. Motivate her to reach new levels of play. She is happy, accomplished and learning invaluable lessons about effort, teamwork, communication and dedication.

Bad coaches can take you to the other extreme.

When it happens to you, it can feel insurmountable, especially for parents. Your child has dedicated hours, days, weeks, months, years... a massive percentage of the early part of her life... to a sport she loves. Then, in one fell swoop, she lands on a team with a "bad" coach. We'll use quotes here out of acknowledgement that everyone views the quality of a coach differently. Some kids may worship the coach that your child dislikes. Maybe it's just a bad fit. Either way, the outcome is the same. What was once a passionate pursuit has become a chore. The sparkle in your daughter's eye is nowhere to be found.

Being assigned to good and bad coaches are completely different situations, right? Of course, the outcomes are, but the root cause is the same. Chance. For the most part, the dynamic between a coach and athlete is unpredictable. Only extended interactions can inform their value.

So, what happens when you realize you have a "bad" coach?

Focus internally
When your child is dealing with this challenge, ask the simple question: Are you playing the sports for your coach, or because you love the game? The answer to this question is telling on many levels. But not defining.

Youth sports is and should be in large part about social connection. Kids want to play with their friends. Sometimes more than the sport itself. And that's ok. It doesn't mean they don't take it seriously. If they play long enough, the priorities may shift. Either way, youth sports can still provide valuable life lessons on the journey to social growth. Playing for external reasons can be ok if they are positive.

Children certainly don't play for external reasons that are negative. They may choose to play on the same team with their friends. If they don't like the players on their team, most likely you'll be looking for a new team.

They can't choose their coaches, however. That external factor can create challenges. Coaches that overemphasize winning will kill the fun. If they rule through negativity, or in other ways that make your child miserable, they will overshadow the joy gleaned from other aspects of participation. But that doesn't mean it's a wash. It simply means you need to focus on internal issues.

If you're stuck with a "bad" coach, the internal focus may be your saving grace. Here are points to discuss with your child:

1) *Focus on the love of the sport.* It may become hard to see. But buried in the pile of soiled frustrations created by the bad coach, there's still the love of the game. Even if it seems otherwise. If the love has completely disappeared, your child wouldn't be playing at all. If she is playing, despite a bad coach, she is fighting to rediscover the love of the game. It may not happen under that "bad" coach, but you can reinforce what's in her control. Think about the game. Visualize the moments that make her happy and seek them out as often as possible.

2) *Focus on your teammates.* If your child is playing sports because of the social hook, double down on it. Instead of playing for a coach, she can play for teammates. Reinforce the merits of camaraderie and teamwork. In fact, if your daughter is being oppressed by the coach, it's likely that some of her

teammates feel the same way. They can use their shared feeling to bond and find a common purpose that can propel them to new heights. Your daughter can find strength in her friends, and together they can make playing on a team the most fulfilling experience of their lives, regardless of the coach.

3) *Hear the feedback.* Even if you have a "bad" coach, there's a good chance that some or even all their critiques have merit. Coaches don't waste their time making a comment unless they believe it will help an athlete improve. Encourage your child to listen to and hear everything that a coach is telling them, emotion free and without judgment. They may not agree and that's ok. They may need time to digest comments. But teaching your kids early in life to collect and assess data, particularly as it pertains to their personal growth, will pay dividends later. They should approach this the same way whether it comes from a good coach or bad coach. They have the right to ultimately decide what value the data has – and either keep or discard it. Either choice is acceptable, if they come to it through reason.

4) *Find other voices.* We've outlined how and why coaching variance occurs. Having good coaches and bad coaches is no different than having good or bad teachers, or good or bad bosses. If you have a bad coach, it's a good idea to find another coach to whom you can listen – possibly through extra training. If you have a great coach, it's still a good idea to find another voice. Limiting exposure to a single coach, in any environment, is dangerous. Find as much information – as many voices – as possible. By collecting data, your child will have the power to evolve more quickly. Yes, there's a risk. Finding a trainer and a second coach for your sports-obsessed child may lead to confusion. How so? Unquestionably, two coaches will give you two different and

conflicting tips on the best technique for striking a soccer ball. That can and will be confusing. But it will also force your kids to understand that there isn't necessarily one right (or wrong) way to do something. It will also force critical thinking and some level of decision-making to settle on which piece of advice is best in such a situation. Adding another voice may also have the power to counteract the negativity imparted by a "bad" coach. There is no downside to finding other voices.

5) *Know it will change.* Because participating in youth sports has become so intense, it's easy to become lost in the immediacy of any situation. There's so much pressure for kids to perform, day in and day out, that the detrimental impact of a "bad" coach feels like the end of the world. When efforts are going backwards, take a deep breath and find some perspective. It's just a game. It's just a moment in time. And it won't last forever. That coach won't always be your coach. Nevertheless, if a coach does happen to stay with a team longer than you want to stay with that coach, your child can leave and find a better situation. We'll get to that soon.

Don't give up trying to break through and develop a good relationship with coaches. Some of the most rewarding relationships start from a challenging place. But, if your child simply has a bad coach, the five concepts above will help you make the most of the situation.

Good parents, bad parents

Here's a tough reality. Just like there are good coaches and bad coaches, there are good parents and bad parents. That's true in the broadest sense of the word, but for the sake of this book, let's stick with sports parenting. Athletes can't control their parents. They also can't control other sports parents.

The same principles about coaches apply to parents as well. Bad sports parents can destroy an athlete's confidence. They can take the fun out of the game. Whether parents are being bad only to their own child or also to other athletes, they can dramatically impact the way a child feels about sports.

Consider the parent on the sidelines barking commands at his son. As he tells his son where to go, what to do and how to do it, is he demonstrating confidence? Does his behavior suggest he believes in his son? With every comment, he erodes his son's self-belief and replaces it with self-doubt.

Kids can't control how parents act on the sideline, just like they can't control the coach of their team. What they can control is how they react to parents. When athletes encounter bad parents, they should apply the same tools described for managing their reaction to bad coaches.

By the way, if you're reading this section and can't figure out which parents would cause that level of angst for young athletes, it's probably you. Take a minute to figure out what kind of parent you want to be. If you're the bad parent, it will be much harder to guide your child through the lessons in this book.

Good teachers, bad teachers
Many of the comparisons we've drawn are school related. Why? Because your child is going through school at the same time she is participating in youth sports. Consequently, there's another great parallel here that she'll experience at the same time.

She can't control the teachers she'll get, and not all will be good.

But if eighth grade brings a bad science teacher, and your daughter loves science, use the behaviors we've noted to get through the year without tearing down a great foundation of passion. Focus on the learning. If she struggles to engage with the teacher, she can double down on the material.

Good bosses, bad bosses

Likewise, as your child starts to explore the working world, this lesson will be uniquely applicable to bosses. Yes, as you're looking for jobs, applicants have some level of control as to where they work. They can choose to apply to multiple opportunities and choose to decline those where the boss may have a bad reputation or seemed like a poor match.

It's not always possible to be that selective. Sometimes, you just need to take the job. When that's the case, identifying appropriate behaviors makes a world of difference. It can make that dreaded job a valuable experience, despite the bad boss.

Good kids, bad kids

We argue above that you can choose a team based on friendships and shift accordingly. True, to a point. For most, making the same decision at a public school is less likely. On a daily basis you are shifted in and out of "teams" on a daily basis – paired with classmates somewhat randomly in different classrooms. For better or worse, these classrooms become the proving grounds for social growth.

Maybe you don't have the good coach and bad coach equivalent with your child's social group. But you certainly have good friends and bad friends. They begin to filter themselves into these groups and you become part of that synthesis.

Searching for one's own identity is challenging. It can be among the most trying times in a young person's life. Doing this as one deals with hundreds of other kids who are also seeking personal clarity, that's even tougher.

As you navigate this labyrinth of emotions, you can't avoid encountering mean kids. At a time when everyone is looking for friendship and acceptance, some children choose a different path. Some kids choose to drive others away or drive them crazy. They're mean. They shirk friendly interactions for confrontational or insulting ones. They overlook kindness and embrace cruelty.

We've all dealt with these people, especially during our school years. They are the jerks. Sometimes they are the popular kid trying to prove something to others; other times, they are the aloof kid with pent up angst. Even if you've avoided this type of negative energy in your own social circles, the gods intervene and force your path to intersect directly with a bad kid.

Maybe this happens to your son. He's in a great place socially. Going through middle school, he has solidified a great group of friends. His group is kind and generous. They are thoughtful and considerate. The growth of his personality reflects his choice of friends, and his choice of friends reflects his core values. In school, he spends as much time with those friends as possible. They all eat lunch together. He has a few classes with each, and when given the opportunity he sits with them. He studies with them.

But in his science class, the teacher is old-school. She assigns seating within the room, then declares the student pairs sitting next to each other will be lab partners. All year long.

Your son is sitting next to a boy named Dennis. He is notorious for being a bad kid. He is the opposite of everything your son has chosen in his friends. Dennis makes jokes at people's expense. He's rude. He's crude. He's inconsiderate. The list goes on. And your son is facing an entire school year where he's stuck working with him. He fears his grades will suffer and his spirits will diminish.

One day after class, during the first week of school, your son approached the teacher asking for a seating change. He expressed his concerns and made his case for a move. The teacher declined. *Not everyone is going to be happy with their seating assignment. It wouldn't be fair to start making changes now, because then other kids will ask. And I can't rearrange everyone based on their requests, or we'll never move on with our curriculum.*

It was settled. Your son had to face the school year stuck with a mean kid. At that moment, he had a choice. Make the most of it, or sulk.

It's worth noting that, if a bad kid crosses over from jerk to bully, it's imperative to find an adult and stop the behavior. Bullying is unacceptable at every stage in life. But if you're just dealing with a mean kid, what then?

Your son can apply the life lessons learned on a soccer field to handle this situation. No, peers aren't coaches. But they are external forces beyond your control that can impact your outlook on life. Dennis had the power to make your son's educational and social experience dramatically different than it may have been with a friend (or good kid) as his year-long lab partner.

So, what's the equivalent?

1) *Focus on learning.* Not everyone enjoys school, but there's invariably something every student can enjoy through learning and engaging in the education process. If your son is challenged by social situations, find the topic that gets him most engaged and dive in. If he doesn't love science, it may be more challenging. But, learning is better than dealing with a mean kid. Focus on his learning. Or consider his work in other classes. Does he love writing? He could write *ad nauseum.* Write about the mean kids. Write about his feelings. Just write if that's the subject he likes most.

2) *Focus on the good teachers.* As noted, the good coach, bad coach premise can apply to teachers. But when you find a good one, he can provide refuge from mean kids. Encourage your son to develop a mentor-type relationship with a teacher that stimulates his interests and to spend more time learning from his life experiences. It may even be the science teacher. She wouldn't change her decision to move your son away from Dennis, but she heard his concerns. She was reasonable. Maybe she will be an exceptional resource as your son navigates the Dennis relationship. Spending time with her might make your son love science. When the bad kids are bothering him, encourage your son to cultivate relationships with his good teachers.

3) *Focus on the good kids.* Easier said than done, but ignore the mean kids and invest energy in those who provide positivity. In more generalized situations, this might be easier. You son can choose where to sit at lunch. Encourage him to choose the people with whom he can talk. If he can't choose – like being partnered with Dennis – he can choose what to do on the fringes. When there is time between lab work, your son can talk to others.

4) *Know it will change.* Growing up is hard. Kids work through understanding their own identity and finding a unique voice. Often, their peers don't even know why they are mean. They may not even intend it. It won't always last. Sure, some kids will never be nice, but relationships will evolve with most. Know that the mean kids may get nicer, or your son can just move on.

This life lesson is about controlling the variables that you can control. In the world of youth sports your coach isn't often one of them. Whether good, or bad, it's critical to accept that and develop behaviors that won't disrupt your passion for playing. Putting the bad coach in perspective will help you when encountering similar situations throughout life.

Good Coaches, Bad Coaches Actions

Of all the anecdotal discussions in this book, the impact of a bad coach is one to which almost everyone can relate. It's also one of the most debilitating scenarios that a sports family can face. The young athlete feels defeated when they are beat down by a bad coach. And parents often feel helpless. In the next chapter we'll explore when it's time to bust through that helpless feeling. But for now, here are some positive actions that can help keep good coaches and bad coaches in perspective.

1. Discuss what really makes a good coach and bad coach so that your young athlete has a clear archetype of each in his mind. Sometimes, a child reacts emotionally to a certain style of coaching. A good coach can feel like a bad coach, and vice versa. The more thoughtful your son's evaluation of the player/coach relationship, the better his judgment will be.

2. Reinforce that all coaches have value, no matter how a player ultimately feels about them. Tune your ear to openly hear critique and assess its value. Coaches always provide another viewpoint for objective feedback.

3. Have your son write down the reasons for playing sports and be sure to read those reasons every time he encounters a bad coach. Make those reasons the focus and control internal variables.

4. Actively seek other voices in a bad coach situation. That may mean that your son spends more time with an assistant coach, outside trainer or knowledgeable parent. Be honest with that person about the situation – that your son is

struggling to connect with a coach – so they understand that you are looking for something different.

5. Try to make it better. That's right, sometimes a bad coach isn't a bad coach at all Instead, the relationship could reflect your own actions. If you feel like the relationship has soured, ask yourself "What can I do to make this better?"

Chapter Fourteen:
The Best Situation

November 5th

Dear Diary,

I have a weird relationship with the idea of "quitting" and its one that I'm sharing often with Kendall right now. No, I don't think you should just quit when you commit to something. But I also think, particularly in the world of sports, the idea of quitting gets a bad rap. It tends to mean you just don't like something, so you're walking away in a huff.

Here's the thing though…as you learn more about any situation, sometimes you figure out that it just may not be right for you. When something's not right for you, doesn't it make sense to evaluate your options? Isn't one of those options always going to be making a change?

In the world of youth sports, if you are on a team that's not good for you – the culture is bad because the girls are mean, or the coach actively speaks to you in a hurtful way – why stay in that situation? It's just like any other evaluation process. If you take a deliberate approach to evaluating something, and decide you're in a bad situation, why wouldn't you change it? Life's too short to stay in a bad situation.

It's not always quitting. Sometimes it's making a better decision. If soccer can teach Kendall to make the best decisions quickly, and either double-down on her investment or move on, that's a good thing.

Sincerely,
Kent (aka, Soccer Dad)

Conventional wisdom

Read about the value of sports, the lessons you're supposed to learn playing games, and you will develop a standard and obvious list. Those include competition, sportsmanship, teamwork, resilience and commitment. Important, sure.

As your child matures, however, the best and most valuable lessons become a bit more nuanced and sophisticated. The increasing intensity of sports participation often makes what we deem the most critical lessons the easiest to overlook. Parents and young athletes alike need to remind themselves that the purpose of playing sports should be grounded in life lessons – the ones we've been talking about throughout this book. Nuanced lessons get lost in an ocean of competition and athletic accomplishments. Find a way to float them to the surface.

What happens, then, when you have that balance and your daughter still isn't feeling content and fulfilled? You are consistently discussing the value of sports off the field, rewarding hard work instead of outcomes and she still seems to be in a bad place? Most likely you've explored the happiness spectrum and it's on the wrong side of the line – your daughter wants to play the sport but isn't having *fun* anymore.

Maybe you think that she is under too much *pressure* at her current club or on a specific team. Yet, she insists that she doesn't feel pressure, though her actual play suggests differently. Maybe that means she plays scared and avoids making mistakes.

Conventional wisdom fails. It's not enriching. It's not the fun. Your child is focused on all the right things, despite having a bad coach but is still not herself on the field. You've tried everything to improve the daily outcomes, but it's not working. She's lost and sad.

What was once fun is now the source if sadness, misery and maybe even depression. When that happens, it's possible your child is on the verge of falling out of love with the sport. Make sure to ask that question and check her mindset.

If she insists that she still loves it, that she's fighting to rediscover her passion for the sport, consider that you may need to make a change. You need to find the best situation to ensure it's all worthwhile.

Examine the situation
Coyle, the brilliant author behind both *The Talent Code* and *The Culture Code,* has spent his life researching and documenting the behaviors required to achieve greatness. The focus of his books is industry-agnostic and does, in fact, deal with exceptional talents and cultures in sports as well as business and other walks of life.

In *The Culture Code*, Coyle establishes three behavioral frameworks required to build elite cultural settings in any organization – vulnerability, safe spaces and common purpose. In all cases, these are established through great leadership.[13] An executive consistently articulates to his team what he doesn't know and makes himself human and relatable to the team. A coach makes it clear to his team that they can take risks on and off the field and will not be punished. Management constantly reminds a company's employees of the medium and long-term goals and how their daily contributions align with achieving them.

Coyle is describing the approach that delivers an opportunity to build exceptional cultures and produce world-class results.

Consider, then, how the opposite can impact your child during her stint on a team.

---

[13] Coyle, Daniel. *The Culture Code: The Secrets of Highly Successful Groups* (New York: Bantam, 2018)

Not only does the coach avoid vulnerability, he articulates a belief that he's never wrong. Do what he says, because he knows best.

The soccer field is not a safe space. In fact, it's the opposite. A place where mistakes are punished in the youth-sports-equivalent of a capital offense – where one is immediately and irrecoverably to the bench.

Common goals, and actions geared towards achieving them, are de-emphasized and individual achievement prioritized. Players attack each other to avoid the appearance of mistakes, blaming one another for small errors during seemingly mundane skill work.

The opposite of good

What if your coach, your team, or your situation is creating the worst possible culture? There is no vulnerability, there is no safety and there's no common purpose.

These are the times when internal focus, as explained in Chapter Thirteen, may simply not be enough. You can't switch your attention to friendships, because they don't exist. The coach is a source of sadness, so too are your teammates.

You can't focus on improving your game because growth comes through mistakes and those are punished.

Even if there was a common goal at that point you probably wouldn't be that interested in finding it. When there's no vulnerability to forge connections, no safety to risk and ultimately make mistakes, the fabric of a good culture is missing. If it's the opposite of those things – though Coyle doesn't say this in his book – it's safe to assume it might be a *bad* culture created by a *bad* coach.

That seems like a bad situation, doesn't? It is, potentially, a scenario where you should immediately look for a better situation.

If your child is playing for a team or club that sounds like this, ask why. Does it reflect your values or contradict them? In life, when you ask and answer those questions, it's typically clear when you should move on. Use the lessons of youth sports to establish the best behaviors for the rest of your life.

When you're in a situation that contradicts your values, find a better situation.

Then what?

That's right, we're suggesting your son *quit*. Yeah, playing sports is supposed to teach persistence and not quitting. But, here's the thing. What's worse? Staying in a situation that is detrimental to your son's personal development and maybe even mental health, so you can say he didn't quit? Or taking thoughtful inventory of the situation and deciding it's wrong for his growth, then moving on?

The definition of insanity, people like to say, is doing the same thing over and over again and expecting a different result. Sports teams practice two or three times a week and then add a game (or two) on top of that. In that scenario, you have the "over and over" again part nailed.

If you watch years of youth sports, you may come to this conclusion – there's only one thing worse than quitting and that's choosing for your son to stay in a toxic situation simply to say he's not a quitter.

Walking away from a bad situation and walking towards a better situation really isn't quitting. It's choosing a better option. We are not suggesting your son walk away from the commitments of the sport. Instead, you're trying to save them if he is walking towards something else. Something healthier. Something you and he both think will be a better situation.

Think of it as stopping something bad and starting something better.

Find a better situation.

Knowing when it's time to move on

This chapter wasn't written without immense consideration. While people are quick to suggest that quitting is the easy way out, getting to the point where you recognize the need to make a change is often immensely difficult.

In the introduction, we explored how Kendall's continued growth as a soccer player led her to PDA, one of the top girls' soccer clubs in the country. However, much of the motivation for this book was watching how increasingly complicated youth sports became during her time there.

During her first year at PDA, she was on the "B" team – the team with the second-best talent – for her age group. They were very good. Her coach was excellent and had a reputation for both winning and developing players. It was intense, but enjoyable. And, as a result, Kendall improved steadily throughout the year. So much so, that she was selected to play on the "A" team – the team with the best talent in the age group – the following year. At first, she was elated. Playing on the top team at a club like PDA is always the goal. As an athlete, you work hard to realize such aspirations.

Rather quickly, however, Kendall sensed that it wasn't the best fit for her personally. The players on the top team had already been together for a few years. They had a tight bond. It was a group widely considered among the most talented, but also most underachieving at the club. She saw why immediately – everyone, she felt, was driven by personal goal. *There was no true common purpose.* Strike one.

Because so much was expected of this group, practices were run with intensity. That was nothing new, but the way her teammates reacted was. Frequently, when a mistake was made, they accusingly would point fingers at one another. Kendall would come home and tell stories of how no one was willing to make a mistake, so when they did, girls were quick to blame one another to deflect. The coach would even side with the "veteran" players over the new ones. *It wasn't a safe place to make mistakes. There was no concept of a growth mindset.* Strike two.

Team leadership didn't exist either. The coach was nice enough, but unable to unify the team. He demanded they spend time together, to forge a sense of camaraderie. But he never organized such efforts. The team captains? They were just eleven years old at the time, and he relied on them to bring the group together. Yet, Kendall would tell stories about how the players would overlook her and others that weren't part of the "in crowd." Typically, players were required to arrive fifteen minutes early for practice. So, everyone would start to gather at 4:45pm for a five o'clock session. Kendall was typically among the first four or five to arrive. Despite that, when the coach would call them in to start and ask who was missing, her name was regularly uttered. The coach didn't correct her teammates. The leaders didn't correct the team. Kendall was invisible and that was acceptable.

The coach and "captains" showed no vulnerability. Strike three. Not only did they blame each other for mistakes, they were never wrong themselves. The coach showed no willingness to demonstrate his shortcomings. He demanded more of the players than he demanded of himself without acknowledging he had room to grow or learn.

For example, they were required to develop ongoing training programs – technical and fitness-based routines intended to ensure improvement outside of practice. So, in addition to two team practices and another one or two games each week, the player was responsible for self-directed improvement. Kendall happily did extra work – she often attended training with a third-party. Maybe as often as twice a week. However, that didn't count towards the regimen. The coach required additional work above and beyond that training.

Worse yet, there was no explanation for what was demanded and why. The players just had to do it because he said so.

Every free minute, of every day, in Kendall's life, was now occupied by soccer. With no real reason. She wasn't given the "why" behind the work. She didn't feel it was making her better.

The fun began to disappear. The passion and drive began to disappear. The willingness to make mistakes began to disappear.

There were many factors. A bad coach, for her. A bad culture, for her. She was in jeopardy of falling out of love with sports and walking away from something that could offer her all the life lessons we're exploring in this book.

Despite the clear struggles, she stuck with it for weeks, then months. With every passing day, she quietly became less interested in going to practice. Less interested in working on her game. Less interested in putting the necessary effort into the game. It had long stopped being the best situation and quickly become a bad situation. It was time to move on. So, after weeks of discussion and deliberation, Kendall left PDA.

Rediscovering fun and passion
It was distinctly out of character for Kendall to walk away from a commitment midseason. It was not, however, unusual for us to seek the best situation for her soccer development. In fact, we had moved several times between local clubs, seeking coaches that believed in and wanted to develop her. Yes, we were that family. The one that everyone thought "jumped around" from team-to-team.

But jumping around was never about finding a "better team." Instead, it was always about finding the best situation for her to have fun, stimulate her passion and continue growing. Truly, it was always that simple. So, we were familiar with the warning signs. Familiar with the variables that indicated a problem. They just didn't always present themselves with the extremity they did at PDA. They were all discussed openly with Kendall along the way.

When she was able to personally articulate that the fun was gone, that the passion was gone, that the willingness to live in a growth mindset was gone, we knew it was time to consider acting.
If she couldn't embrace and learn from her experiences, what was the point? If she was going to quit soccer, did it matter if she "stuck it out" with her team? It's all about perspective.

Ultimately, it's about the best situation
We heard the voices...

> *Don't quit now (because you've committed to this team)*
> *Don't quit now (because a parent tells you to see it through)*

But listening to each of these voices could have negative consequences.

The smartest people are constantly collecting data and correcting their course. Youth sports doesn't have to be any different. It was time to move on.

Our goal, then, was to continue looking for the best situation for Kendall to reclaim those concepts. During the spring season, she played with a local club where she knew and liked the other players. She also tried out for additional teams with the following season in mind. It was a process. Every time we collected data and evaluated the best move for the future, we asked consistent questions.

> *Do you think you'll have fun there?*
> *Will you want to put in the work for that team?*
> *How does the culture seem?*
> *Does the coach create an environment where you are comfortable failing?*

At no point did we focus on picking the best team. The one that would win trophies. Sure, that would be nice. But it wasn't the objective. She made her decisions exclusively with one goal in mind – to enjoy soccer so she could maximize the time she spent playing it.

A new dance studio, too

It also happened with Hayden. As she became increasingly serious about dance, her fun, passion and drive were all attached to improvement. She loved to dance, and she took immense pride in studying her craft.

As an ambitious ten-year-old, she wanted to be dancing with teenagers. The idea was to test herself daily and find ways to make mistakes, then improve.

She also aspired to earn a competition solo.

But, despite spending several years as a promising dancer at her studio, she hit a wall. She felt the opportunities to test herself were minimal. That limited her fun and minimized her growth.

She felt the studio's leaders lacked vulnerability. There was no discernible drive for them to improve. They consistently settled for the same approach and results. Every year.

Like Kendall, Hayden felt that she wasn't in the best situation and she moved on. Many of her friends didn't understand because they couldn't do the same thing. Why? Because the best situation for them was one of social stability. They didn't want to leave friends. They were far less concerned with improvement.

When Hayden questioned the situation, it concerned improvement. She wasn't quitting her studio, she was moving on to another studio.

Life's too short for dead-end jobs

How often do adults get stuck in jobs? We are taught as children, over and over, to pursue a career path driven by passion for a chosen field. As we move through school, acquiring degrees, that drive seems to vanish. It's replaced by the need to find an income, develop financial independence and create some level of stability. Because passion-based pursuits can take time, they often take a back seat to a salary-generating job.

Over time, such decisions wear on you. Four years of college English, full of creative writing, gets filed away in the memory banks. The stories you wrote get filed away in an archive folder. The written word is replaced by GANTT charts and web-based project management software.

For four years, you thrived in an environment where professors showed consistent vulnerability. Where you were in the best place to make mistakes. Where students have common goals of intellectual growth. Then you move into an office where terrorizing bosses crush all of these behaviors. But you need the income.

This is the time when you need to learn from the life lessons of youth athletics, and model behavior for your children. Apply the best situation principle to your work life.

If you find yourself ten or twenty years into a career and can't find fun on a day-to-day basis, re-assess the type of work you are doing.

Conversely, if you like the type of work you're doing, but not where you're doing it, ask key questions. Is your environment devoid of vulnerable leadership, a scenario that encourages growth and a peer group that lacks a common goal? You may be in the wrong place.

This doesn't have to apply only to the corporate world. The same criterion should be considered if your daughter has enough time outside of school and sports to get a job at the local ice cream parlor. If she can't find fun, or a growth-oriented setting, it's probably not the best situation.

Think about Rick Ankiel, not Rudy

A final thought on this topic. Pop culture puts the spotlight on perseverance. It highlights the guy that fights to overcome everything and reach his goal. Rarely do we see the story of a "quitter" given the attention it deserves.

Take, for example, the story of Daniel Eugene "Rudy" Ruettiger. He famously dreamed of playing football at the University of Notre Dame, despite being just 5'6" and 165 pounds. Rudy was neither a good enough football player nor student to earn admission to Notre Dame. But he worked relentlessly to make his way to the college, then worked his way on the football team's practice squad and eventually earned a few minutes of playing time on the field. The story became so renowned, that a motion picture, starring Sean Astin, was made about Rudy's experience. Over time, it became something of a cult classic.[14]

Rudy didn't become a professional. He just had a feel-good story. But the underlying determination made the story worthy of a movie. The "don't quit" lesson made Rudy's story famous.

While many people have heard of Rudy because of the movie, few know of Rick Ankiel. His professional sports aspirations took a very different path than Rudy's. Drafted by the St. Louis Cardinals in 1997, Ankiel was so talented that he reached the Major League level just two years later in 1999. The following year, he racked up 194 strikeouts and 11 wins, showing the type of talent that earned him

---

[14] Dan Scofield, "Daniel "Rudy" Ruettiger, Notre Dame's Famous Walk-On: The True Story," *Bleacher Report*, January 18, 2010, https://bleacherreport.com/articles/328263-the-true-story-of-notre-dames-famous-walk-on-daniel-rudy-reutigger.

universal praise. He was on track to become a star.

There was nothing that could stop him.

Except, then it all fell apart. The Cardinals made the playoffs and Ankiel was expected to play a critical role in the team's success. What followed is one of the most famous cases of the "yips" – when an athlete seems to just forget how to perform a particular primary skill like throwing a baseball – in modern sports history. Ankiel could no longer control his pitches – throwing five wild pitches in one inning during his first start. He basically repeated the feat in his second start. He had lost his ability to pitch in the blink of an eye.

Rudy's story tells us that Ankiel should have persevered! That's what sports heroes do. And he tried. Between 2001 and 2005 he attempted to work through his challenges and become the pitcher everyone once believed was destined for greatness.

But then he made a choice. Ankiel decided to walk away from a bad situation and walk towards a better one. A gifted athlete in every way, Ankiel earned a chance to play professional baseball at a different position with the Cardinals. In 2006, he improbably tried to switch from pitcher to outfielder at the highest level of the sport.

By 2008, he had once again reached the Major League level. Over the next few years, Ankiel established himself as a legitimate everyday player. He battled some injuries and moved to five more teams before retiring after the 2013 season.[15]

Yes, Ankiel quit pitching when he faced struggles. That's the opposite of what movies tell us should happen. But, he made the right decision. He left a bad situation – one that would have driven

---

[15] Ankiel, Rick and Tim Brown. *The Phenomenon: Pressure, the Yips, and the Pitch that Changed My Life* (New York: Hatchette Book Group, 2017)

him out of baseball forever – to find a better situation.

In doing so, Ankiel reclaimed a dream that had evaded him. His story is one of finding the best situation.

It's something all young athletes should strive to do. Parents need to help. If soccer can teach this lesson during childhood, your child will have the courage to find a better situation throughout life.

Best Situation Actions

Society has obfuscated the concept of quitting. A stigma has been attached to those that walk away from something, particularly in sports. To be sure, there are quitters. People that simply don't want to do the work, and then choose to walk away instead. But, that's not what we're talking about here. Instead, we are encouraging a methodical approach to decision-making – specifically choosing to walk away from a bad situation and walk towards a better one. The following five actions will reinforce examination and exploration of the best situation.

1. Define the values that drive youth athletics for your child. In this chapter, we use fun and team cultural elements as key drivers in Kendall's story. But every athlete has a different reason for playing. Know your child's reason and make sure to evaluate the situation against those values.

2. Describe what good looks like, then describe what the best situation looks like. It's easy to react emotionally to a difficult situation – bad coach, bad teammates, etc. – but comparing that scenario to your definition of "good" or "best" can be enlightening. Things may not be as bad as they seem, particularly by your personal standards.

3. Give it time, but a specific amount of time. Many good situations seem bad at the outset. If you completed action number two, and still conclude you truly are not in a good

or the best situation, settle on that conclusion then "sleep on it" as they say. Maybe for a week, a month or two months. But give it time to ensure you aren't walking away before improvement can occur.

4. Actively talk to athletes on other teams, at other clubs and beyond. Ask them about their situation. Gauge how a situation fits your values based on those conversations before you choose a new club or team. Do your research so you don't find yourself back in a bad situation again.

5. Define the best situation for other aspects of your life – school, career aspirations, social life, etc. Write this down and return to it anytime you feel like you've deviated from a path of excellence. Sports can teach you that the best situation stimulates growth specific to, and unrelated to a craft.

Chapter Fifteen:
More than Soccer

November 12th

Dear Diary,
The fall soccer season is winding down. There have been a lot of ups and downs these past few months. While it hasn't always been easy, soccer keeps giving us lessons that Kendall can take far beyond the field.

What a gift that has been. When you start focusing on the life lessons that soccer can bring, soccer becomes much more fun. Maybe that's because you stop focusing on the game, which lets it become fun again. Maybe it's because kids sense that they really should be playing sports for reasons that have nothing to do with sports. It's fulfilling for them when you choose to go through that journey instead of a different one.

Whatever the case, the last few months have reminded me that playing soccer is about a lot more than soccer. The lessons Kendall learns are building her character in a way that extends beyond competition and teamwork. Sure, those are important, but when every touch of a soccer ball can bring her closer to being a better friend, manager and leader (or so many other things) focusing on that is the key.

Yep, I knew it once before, when I reflected on my baseball career… playing sports is about more than sports. But with Kendall, remembering that it's about more than soccer has been a gift.

Sincerely,
Kent (aka, Soccer Dad)

It's all just a game

Ultimately, participating in youth sports is great. It's rewarding, fulfilling and memorable. But it's critical to never lose perspective. There is more to life than soccer (or baseball, or tennis, or field hockey, or football... you get the idea). Every single day, it's important to remind yourself of this and remind your child even more.

One of the last lessons we'll emphasize is that sports can teach your child that everything we do in life is really a game. We're all just organisms trying to have fun.

If we take life too seriously or put too much emphasis on any one pursuit or endeavor, we lose perspective of what's most important.

Using sports to de-emphasize sports

The great thing about the time spent playing sports is that it lends itself to focusing on everything else. If you consider where we've emphasized teachable moments, many are off the field, outside of the sidelines.

Why? Consider how much of your commitment to sports occurs on the field, then compare it to the amount of time spent in the car or at home. Consider the dynamics of the relationship between you and your young athlete. Where are you interacting with them? Not on the field. When you truly think about how you interact with your child, the time and place to discuss critical life lessons becomes rather clear.

Use a methodical approach to get the most out of this exercise. Here's a suggested progression as you try to focus youth sports on life lessons.

1) *Use this book.* This entire book is focused on finding the most important life lessons in playing a game. Review the

concepts and then, instead of internalizing and practicing them on your child, explicitly discuss and emphasize them with your child. Let them in on the secret that you're actively focused on changing how you approach the family's investment in youth sports.

2) *Use your drive time.* Yep, we recommended a better way to handle sports conversation during the drives to and from practices and games. But this is a treasure trove of the world's most valuable commodity – time. Put it to good use.

Have you asked your son about his classes recently? His relationships with his teachers? Are you up to speed on what his friends are doing with their time? You may think you know what his goals and aspirations are – academically, athletically, etc. – but it never hurts to review them.

The best way to demonstrate that there's more to life than just sports is to act on it. Talk about other stuff.

3) *Emphasize the fringe benefits.* Early in her soccer career, Kendall observed that soccer could take her places. Not figuratively – she wasn't focused on the potential fame or (relative) financial gain associated with professional athletics. It was much more literal. She saw that soccer, as a global sport, often sent athletes around the world in the name of competition. And it starts early. Elite clubs begin traveling across the United States when kids are twelve and thirteen. Those same clubs, as well as Olympic Development Programs (ODP), feature international trips starting at the same ages. Kendall's aspirations to travel have nothing to do with soccer – she's a Francophile, lover of America's Pacific Northwest, intrigued by Italy and more. But maybe soccer could give her the chance to travel… now that's interesting for reasons that have nothing to do with her on-

field performance. Focus on these various reasons your child plays soccer that have nothing to do with the sport.

4) *Play other sports.* Wait, are we suggesting the best way to de-emphasize sports is by playing more sports? Sort of. Really, the insight here is to stay away from specialization in the name of balance, fun and diversity. This chapter is called "More than Soccer," and that's exactly it. By encouraging your child to play multiple sports, there will be an opportunity to learn different skills and crafts, with different people and varying experiences. It will give your child options. It will create distractions, between one sport and another. It will help keep everything in perspective.

5) *Reward the work.* Motivating your child to excel in a sport is most effective when you reward the effort, not the outcomes. It's true even if you're just trying to use sports to focus on other areas of life. A focus on process and pursuit, and then the passion that fuels it, translates to every facet of life. After you leave the playing field and pursue science, sales or sailing... focusing on process over the outcomes will pay off.

6) *Focus on the funny.* Crazy stuff happens when kids play sports. A baseball falls past their glove and hits them in a chin, they slip on a wet field and fall on their back trying to tackle someone, or they completely miss a golf ball on the first tee. When these things happen, laugh. Remind them it's just a game and, ultimately, doesn't matter. But also remind them that growth comes from making mistakes. Blooper reels are awesome and as memorable than great feats.

Spend time on school

One of the great enigmas surrounding the modern sports parent is the importance put on sports as a priority over everything else. Most families don't stop to consider just how great the investment is and how that investment impacts their lives.

Let's do some math.

- Your soccer team practices twenty minutes away. Round trip, that's forty minutes.
- Practice is twice a week. So, before you ever play a game, you've committed to one hour and twenty minutes of driving.
- If you travel for games, assume an average of thirty minutes in each direction and you're now at two hours and twenty minutes total time spent in one week.

That's just commuting time.

Do you help your child get dressed for the activities? Get water? Even if it's a minimal investment, say ten or fifteen minutes per event, you're up to three hours per week.

Be honest with yourself. Do you spend three hours a week supporting their academic pursuits? Probably not.

Have you stopped to ask yourself why?

Ironically, for most parents, it's because they have placed all their hopes at a college coupon, not on academics, but on sports. So, they spend little to no time focusing on education, instead obsessed with sports, so that athletic achievement can earn them, what, a free education? That's an odd and unnavigable circular dependency. It's also sad.

When you do that financial math, it becomes clearer that youth sports spend is more like buying a lottery ticket than making an investment. Most kids simply won't earn a college sports scholarship.

Spend as much time pursuing stretch goals
Maybe your child is already a great student on her own. Awesome! That gives you more time to do something else with your non-sports focus.

Make no mistake. That's exactly what you should do. Don't revert to your habit of talking sports, when homework is a non-starter or a non-problem. Find stretch goals to discuss.

Have you asked what careers interest your child? Maybe they are too young to have thought about it. Kendall is great at math and science, so every few weeks we discuss robotics, computer programming and earth sciences. Not extensively, because that requires expertise. But maybe that's the very expertise that she would develop if we explore such interests.

If it's too early to talk about traditional careers, cultivate an interest in starting a lemonade stand, lawn service or dog walking business.

The parallels to sports are amazing. Starting a home-based business requires commitment, persistence and often teamwork. Like sports can teach your child valuable lessons, so too can the effort to earn money. Yes, that's a different book. But for the sake of this book, it's a fantastic companion to your youth sports energy.

Try it out.

What's the point of life?
No, we're not trying to answer life's big question in this youth sports-focused book. But if you're looking for a simple application of this life lesson, look no further.

Youth sports is about more than soccer – it teaches your child about himself, about how to interact with others, about how to grow as a person.

The same can be said for other endeavors. If your child dances, then use the concepts in this book as a framework for her personal growth through dedication to an activity.

Remember, there's more than soccer.

More than Soccer Actions

How do you maximize participation in youth sports? By focusing on other things. Not while your child is on the field, but with the countless hours dedicated to sports elsewhere – in the car, at home, etc. Explore the actions below to make sure you're getting more than soccer out of your child's participation in soccer.

1. Use this book to emphasize the life lessons your family can take away from youth sports participation. If you actively prioritize the non-sports values of sports, the lessons become clearer to everyone.

2. Detail the fringe benefits of sports. Kendall wanted to use sports to travel. If soccer or other sports affords this opportunity, consider taking the whole family on soccer trips. Experience new cultures and then talk about them as a family. Make sure you learn along the way. Becoming more cultured and educated because you daughter can kick a soccer ball is awesome.

3. Make a list of topics you want to explore with your child – school, hobbies, etc. – and make them a priority during your drive to and from the field. This is valuable talk time. Use it to the fullest.

4. Explore stretch goals. Your son spent six hours a day in school, two hours playing soccer and another two hours doing homework. There's still time to start a side business, if that's a stretch goal interest. Shift the car ride

conversations to business planning and you're well on your way.

5. Don't take any of it too seriously. Chapter One is about ensuring "fun" is part of the equation. When all is said and done, we should find the fun in everything we do. Find a smile or laugh in every soccer situation because, well, there's more to life than soccer.

Chapter Sixteen:
Better Than You

November 17th

Dear Diary,
Ultimately, I only want one thing for Kendall (and Hayden) – to have the best life possible, including anything and everything she gets out of her time playing sports. That's the same thing all parents want, right?

When it comes to sports, it doesn't always seem that way. But the more I've focused on life lessons from soccer, the more I just want her to have a better experience than I had playing baseball.

Maybe she will play professionally or maybe she will stop playing next year. That's not what I mean about her having a better experience. I want her to find richness and fulfillment in every minute she spends on a soccer field, which I didn't.

I want her to focus on building great behaviors and a strong character. If she focuses on those goals rather than sports-specific ones, she will do it better than I did.

It's been a fun ride, but with the season coming to an end, my entries might trail off a bit. But, more to come soon.

Sincerely,
Kent (aka, Soccer Dad)

Why sports?

So much of this book was motivated by watching dysfunction around youth sports. It exists in any number of places and has become the norm more than the exception.

Kids feel pressure to perform at too young an age, forced into specialization before it makes sense. They burn out, stop having fun and ultimately quit playing what they once loved.

Parents live vicariously through their children. They long for the euphoric feeling of on-field excellence and urge their kids to work relentlessly to achieve a level they likely never did. It's classic misguided energy. Unquestionably, they are not focused on the child's best interests.

Parents may also believe that playing sports is their child's ticket to a free college education. They encourage giving up the fun of childhood to *potentially* become good enough to earn an athletic scholarship. Which in turn, often means they are committing their college life to sports. Of course, these may be the ambitions for some kids. But for many, it's not. Instead, parents push.

Did your parents push you? Did you pursue your dreams freely? If not, don't you want better for your kids? Even if you did have your parents support, could it have been better? Don't you still want better for your kids?

Don't you want them to go through life better than you did, whatever that means? That should apply to their relationship with sports as well.

What does "better" mean?

As a parent, you should want your child to excel on the sports field. And you should want them to be better than you.

But, that may mean different things for them than it did for you.

"Better than you" doesn't necessarily mean they exceed your on-field accomplishments. If it's your child's goal, that would be outstanding. If your child excels, that's great too. Maybe they can become the superstar you never were. If your son decides he wants to play professional sports, and you didn't, then that could certainly be one way in which he achieves more than you.

In general, however, better performance must be measured on a scale that children determine for themselves. Remember that chapter, "Not Everyone Scores Goals?" You should keep that one in mind. Maybe you were a goal scorer. But embrace your daughter's passion for playing defense, and then want her to be more passionate about defense than you were about scoring.

On the other hand, maybe it means they developed better work ethic or social balance than you did. Those are their goals, and you need to support them. In those cases, it's about the experience and the resulting life lessons. *You need to want their experience to be better than yours.* Even if you had a great experience.

On their terms
At very least, you should aspire for your children to play youth sports on their terms. That means they define the relationship they want to have with sports – whatever that may be – and then achieve the relationship they define.

It's fair to assume that most people – maybe you included – never had the relationship with sports that they wanted. You weren't as good as you hoped. Parents didn't support your goals. Your career ended because you were cut from a team and chose to no longer play. Or your career ended due to injury, one from which you never recovered.

"Better than you" can simply mean that your child gets exactly what he wanted out of it. Simple aspiration, right?

Better for you, too
Truly and completely embodying this concept means understanding what's best for your children will also be best for you. If they are happy, your relationship will thrive. If they achieve desired balance, it should make you happy. That happiness will result in a better relationship between you. Ultimately, that will make all the time and effort spent on youth sports very worthwhile.

College isn't for everyone
If you accept that "better than you" doesn't necessarily mean professional sports, then there's a world of opportunity for you and your child to apply life lessons to other areas.

One of the great clichés is that every generation wants to leave the world in a better place for the next generation. But, often, that's measured by advances in medicine, technology, and financial splendor. Instead, we should be measuring that in happiness and fulfillment.

For example, you often hear the idea that it's important for your child to attend a better college than you. Just as your parents wanted for you. Why? Typically, the more education you complete, the better your earning potential is. Moreover, the better college or graduate school you attended, the better job you are bound to get. The value of education has historically been compounded by the brand name on your degree(s).

Changing times and paradigms have de-emphasized, though not eliminated, the direct correlation between education, brand and success. If we're honest, it was never directly correlative. Many high-school dropouts worked their way to business success. Many college dropouts found their path.

Consider that college isn't for everyone, and that "everyone" could easily include your child. "Better than you" may mean they happily skip college to pursue other passions, instead of struggling through four years of accounting classes to earn a degree that locks them into a job they never wanted, but their father told them was necessary.

Sam's story

Sam was an outstanding student. She earned straight "A's" through high school and added dance, theater and other activities to her resume. Her older sister, also a model student, attended Temple University in Philadelphia. And, Sam was potential Ivy League material.

At least, according to her parents. Sam had different ideas. After watching her older sister struggle during her first year at Temple, Sam wondered whether her sister had been ready to attend college. Whether she had a guiding principle that informed the classes she took and dictate a long-term purpose. Or whether entering college without a clear plan had caused her to struggle.

Sam then asked the same questions of herself. Why was she going to college, and what did she want to do? Introspection led to clarity. She didn't have a clear path of study. When she imagined happiness, the image that formed in her head featured designing costumes and sets on Broadway.

Would four-years at a top private school and seven-figures of debt lead her to Broadway as a professional costume designer? Not likely.

Why then follow the expected path and go to college when that wasn't her best life? There was no rule that said she had to go to college right after high school. Colleges weren't going anywhere. Sam ultimately chose to take a year off before considering college, so she could more deeply explore her passions. That wasn't the same path her sister took. Nor was it the same path her parents took. But it obtained a better outcome, for her, because she wasn't ready to embrace and maximize the college experience.

The entire time, her mother, Claire, stood by supporting the decision. Why? Well, college had been a mixed bag for Claire. In truth, Claire had the same doubts when she left home thirty years before. So, watching Sam explore her relationship with education and its outcomes meant Sam would have a better experience.

How can you ensure that your child's experience is better than yours? That's ultimately the goal. Manage that emotional relationship with soccer and you'll be building a model for other aspects of life.

Better than You Actions

Are your kids better than you at sports? Before you answer, it's critical to know exactly what that means. How do you define "better?" Is it the skills, the experience, the outcome or something else? In this chapter, we've reviewed how to let your child determine their relationship with sports, then allowing them to develop it exclusively on their terms. That should make them happy and fulfilled in ways you never experienced. Here are some actions to help reach that point.

1. Other books will tell you to set goals with your son regarding his participation in sports. We're doing the same thing, but without focusing on the individual or team success on the field. Instead, identify the macro-level goals for your son – does he want to play just a few years, casually, competitively, etc. Or is he looking to use sports to improve other aspects of his life? Whatever the goal, make sure you define it. Then revisit it and refine it, ensuring that he controls his relationship with those goals.

2. Actively define all the outcomes related to those goals and choose which will make your child happiest. Work towards

happiness as the ultimate outcome, which may bring the value of other activities and benefits into focus.

3. Share your own sports stories with your child. Focus on the things that went poorly and talk about how you wish you had managed your relationship with youth sports differently. Showing vulnerability through your previous experiences will make it easier for your child to share his true goals.

4. Carry the three steps above into other aspects of your child's life. How can he be better than you in every aspect of what he does?

5. Repeatedly question whether you're putting too much value on the outcomes of your son's activities. Is that conducive to him having better experiences than you had? It's not about you, it's about your child.

Part Four:
Wrapping Up

*(Applying the Concepts and
Looking for More)*

Chapter Seventeen:
Life Lessons Everywhere

November 28th

Dear Diary,
A funny thing happened this week. I started seeing the same patterns that we've been talking about for the last few months emerge around Hayden's experience in dance. And Cindy's experience at her job.

Pretty much everywhere, really.

The realization? There are life lessons everywhere. Every experience can help you learn about yourself and the world around you in a way that applies to every other part of your life. You don't have to hide on the sidelines to find them, they are right in front of you.

Sports can help you become a better business person.
Arts can make you a better scholar.
Cooking can teach you to be a better parent.
Parenthood can make you a better coach.

No matter what you do, the focus should remain on learning about yourself, your family, your friends and the world around you. Then apply lessons learned in one area to another. Think of it as behavioral cross training. If you can do that, you just might find a balance worth keeping.

Thanks for listening these last few months. I think we've talked about some great topics

Sincerely,
Kent (aka, Soccer Dad)

What's the point?

There were a few motivations for this book. The first was to take a different approach to restoring order to youth sports. The "adultification" of youth sports has, in many ways, destroyed its joy for our kids. Parental expectations, involvement and, frankly, insanity, have taken the fun out of *games*.

As a result, increasing numbers of kids give up *participation in sports for life* by the age of thirteen.[16] What a shame. Why do our kids feel like they have to quit sports to avoid the negative energy associated with playing?

The idea here, then, is to accept that parents will become invested in their kids' activities. It's unavoidable. It's also clear that the change in intensity of participation is not likely to reverse itself. Parental involvement is not a bad thing if directed appropriately.

That's where we hope this book comes in. Instead of asking parents to limit or even eliminate their involvement, we've suggested redirecting that energy – focus on the broader life lessons associated with youth sports.

Instead of worrying about your child's athletic talent, worry about his ability to create enduring value around everything soccer-related, day-after-day.

For example, if you and your child focus more on learning how to communicate than you do on learning how win, the long-term value will be greater to you both.

That's it. That's been the entire goal of this book. If you've taken

---

[16] Kelly Wallace, "How to make your kid hate sports without really trying" *CNN.*, January 21, 2016, https://www.cnn.com/2016/01/21/health/kids-youth-sports-parents/index.html

even just a little of that away from your time reading, then we know the world of youth sports is better for it. You're better for it. Your child is better for it.

If we've made a small difference in your approach, we're headed in the right direction.

It's not just soccer

This mindset is not unique to youth soccer or youth athletics. Ultimately, here's the thing: you can improve your approach to life through every action you take. Find the perspective that you're seeking and attack what you do through that lens.

Does art interest you? Sure, take it seriously and make it a priority to develop drawing or painting skills. More importantly, approach it with passion and drive. Embrace making mistakes. Know your position (a specific medium, maybe?) and then another (a secondary medium to enhance your overall aesthetic).

Want to start a business? Be the chauffeur – set the goals for the business then get great people to attack them by showing them the route but letting them get out at the stops. Be a good front-seat coach along the way – once you give them the autonomy, let them execute without micromanaging. Want your employees to be better than you – hiring top talent will move you towards having a top company.

These life lessons apply everywhere. Every single day.

What can other activities teach you?

The life lessons in this book are those that soccer is teaching us, and that we encourage you to learn. But our art and business examples may have other life lessons embedded in them that extend this list. Use this book as a framework and apply it to your child's other endeavors.

If the lessons associated with starting a business – passion, drive, grit – seem like the wrong list or a subset of the more important list, seek a deeper understanding. Find the real-life lessons associated with that and anything else your child does.

Life lessons are everywhere. What are you waiting for? Go find them.

Chapter Eighteen:
Diary of a Soccer Dad Actions

November 24th

Dear Diary,
I was reading over my old entries and realized how many lessons we talked about this season! There are too many to remember, so I'm going to write them down in one place.

That should make it easy to review them when things get a little confusing along the way.

Let's hope it helps.

Sincerely,
Kent (aka, Soccer Dad)

Everything old is new again
If you're interested in taking action to enforce the life lessons we've learned, but don't feel like re-reading each chapter, look no further. This section is a quick reference collection of the actions outlined at the end of each chapter. Enjoy.

Chapter One
Fun Actions
Sports experiences can teach us that fun is the foundation on which all other life lessons are built. Here are five key actions that will help keep fun in focus. They apply to athletics and other activities for your kids.

1. Talk about what specifically makes a sport fun for your child. Ask what is the most fun aspect of her participation on a day-to-day basis. How can she maximize those specific elements?

2. Explore the opposite side of that equation. What are the least fun parts of sports or other activities? How can you work to minimize those?

3. Identify where your child seems to have hit a wall. Find out what fun growth opportunities may reinvigorate him. For your child-athlete, is it an experience, travel, a second sport, spiritual activity, or something else? For a student, is it extra emphasis on one subject without concern for another? More reading? Finding a tutor?

4. Integrate fun activities into routine. Fun shouldn't be a one-off situation. Organizing an event specifically built around fun can help.

5. As a parent, make sure you're having fun. Behavior is modeled and if you can't enjoy yourself, it may be hard for

your child to do so. Go through the exercises above, pointed inward.

Chapter Two
Passion and Drive Actions
If you're fortunate enough to watch passion and drive motivate your child's pursuit of youth athletics, take note. Observe the behavior, praise it and reward it. Most likely, life once gave you a taste of passion and drive. Remind yourself of that time and recapture it, for yourself and others.

1. Learn your child's fun-to-passion spectrum. What makes things fun and where does that lead to passion? Where is it just fun for the sake of fun? Where you see the passion, build a series of goals.

2. Actively define "passion and drive" in the context of goals. Working hard doesn't mean working all the time. But it does mean working with clarity, consistency and purpose. Know that excellence is the end goal, not time spent. Decide what the right level of drive is to achieve those goals.

3. Take a temperature check along the way. Find ways to gauge progress, then use them to reaffirm that passion and drive are being applied to the right things and are working.

4. Remind yourself that passions can change and when they do, it's ok. Specific drive can disappear if the passion dissipates. Passion and drive take significant effort, so be sure to put it in the right place.

5. Reward the behavior of passion and drive repeatedly. The outcomes don't matter because the behavior will lead to amazing things – you just may not know which application will be the ultimate one.

Chapter Three
Make Mistakes Actions

How can you focus on cultivating a growth mindset? All of the behaviors explored in this book have challenges and this is among the most challenging of the group. While we provide actions for exploring each life lesson and influencing behaviors to empower young athletes and parents alike, the freedom to make mistakes requires constant action. Here are some that will help.

1. This is going to seem simple, but talk about the value of making mistakes. Sometimes perfectionists – those that hate mistakes the most – are among the most analytical people around. Working through the logic of error and the value of a growth mindset will give them the resources needed to adopt it.

2. Fear is typically the emotion blocking failure. Find and explore examples of failure that have resulted in dramatic growth. Two sports examples immediately come to mind – basketball legend Michael Jordan being cut from his high school basketball team and all-time great quarterback Tom Brady falling to pick 199 in the NFL draft. If "failure" can drive two sports legends, it can help you.

3. Modeling behavior is critical. Share your own vulnerabilities as a parent with your child. Then show them how you will push yourself to make mistakes in your own life and grow from them.

4. Focus on one area of growth, not many. While it's great to make mistakes, going from perfectionist to a person who wants to fix "everything" is impossible. Focusing on an area of particular apprehension – just one – and overcoming the fixed mindset will unlock doors. Stay focused.

5. Recalibrate after you've mastered something that was once a stretch. Just because a specific growth opportunity becomes an area of mastery doesn't mean the behavior should end. Find the next place where mistakes will become the tools for growth and focus energy there.

Chapter Four
Chauffeur Actions
How can you become a great chauffeur? The behaviors related to this life lesson are tough for some to practice because they require patience. For "Type A" personalities, keeping your eyes on the road and hands on the wheel, while passengers plot the tactical future, can be a unique challenge. But, embracing this role can be among the most rewarding in a sports parent's life.

1. Make sure you really know the destination. This sounds silly, but it takes preparation. Too often soccer parents don't double check the location of a game or practice. It shows preparation and commitment. You can only be a great chauffeur if you know where you're actually taking your passenger.

2. Get comfortable with silence. Once you buy into the notion that driving your passenger to the designated destination requires parallel performance – you getting there and her getting ready for what happens once you get there – you realize that silence is productive.

3. Prepare for empathy. Know where your passenger is going and consider the potential outcomes at the destination to which you've driven. What could go wrong and how can you demonstrate an emotional connection to the situation. If you're not prepared, you are likely to have your own reaction instead of relating to hers.

4. Similarly, know what outcomes you should reward. Your passengers will be focused on outcomes, which is awesome. But when things go right, you have a fantastic opportunity as the chauffeur to reinforce the life lessons we're exploring in this book. When your passenger scores a goal, consider the rewards and recognition should be focused on the passion and drive that got them to this point.

5. Practice over-communicating when you're not driving. The only way to give plenty of information at the right time is to become the type of person that gives it all of the time. Chauffeurs over communicate when they're not in the car, so it's easier to stay silent when they are in the car.

Chapter Five
Front Seat Coaching Actions
It would be easy to say, "just don't front-seat coach." But when the reality of emotional intervention is such an obvious obstacle, it's easier to arm yourself with actions that empower you to be a *good* front-seat coach. Here are five things to consider.

1. Review the previous chapter and become a great chauffeur. Yes, there's much more to be done with drive time than remaining silent. But if you start with empathy, rewards/recognition and recharging, then just embrace silence, you'll be better off than a front-seat coach. Be a great chauffeur before you tailor the rest of your front-seat persona.

2. Practice silence. This may be the toughest behavior to embrace, but potentially the most important. When you're a silent front-seat coach, that's when your child can recharge. This is a critical action for you to take.

3. Make a list of the non-sports items you don't get to talk about with your child. Whatever ends up on that list, choose one for every drive and make it a topic of conversation.

4. Study a craft (sports, job roles, etc.) enough to talk about it on a macro-level. If it's soccer, be prepared to talk about professional athletes and their exploits. If it's graphic design your child loves off the field, learn about a few great designers. Either way, study so you can speak from a place of more authority.

5. Remind yourself before and after games to reward the right behaviors. No matter the outcome of a game, if you're telling your son that you're proud of his passion and drive, you're reinforcing big picture lessons.

Chapter Six
Not Everyone Scores Goals Actions
Wanting the spotlight is natural. It's an easy way to feel accepted, appreciated and adored. So many aspire to take on the leading role. As a society, we don't place enough value on the less visible jobs that carry as much meaning and substance. Sadly, glamourizing a few specific actions and ignoring those that perform important work starts at places like the youth soccer field. There are many ways to emphasize the importance of those who don't score goals. Here are some actions to put this behavior into practice.

1. Identify and discuss all of the roles on a team. Dive deep into how each on contributes to the group's overall success. You and your child have to know and understand the importance of everyone – goals scorers and beyond – to combat the notion that only one person is important.

2. Explore the types of contributions that make your son happy. What does he believe his special gift is on the playing

field? If it's scoring goals, that's great! But maybe he loves to pass, or he wants to be a goalkeeper. In other sports, consider the same questions. In school, also take this approach. If he loves art, or math, or social studies understand why and embrace how those skills can make him a unique and critical contributor to various groups.

3. Celebrate the accomplishments of everyone, even the least visible contributors. As a parent, modeling this behavior will let your child know that you mean what you say and that you truly value those with the more subtle but important roles. Two things happen with this. First, your child will feel more comfortable stepping into roles to which he aspires. Second, he will become a better teammate by pointing out those contributions to others.

4. Actively discuss team dynamics in all walks of life. Ensure you're seeking a deeper understanding of the contributions of each team member, regardless of the setting. This type of cross-training will benefit your daughter on and off the field.

5. Reflect on the various roles you've played throughout your life – either in sports, business, or the family. Go through the same exercise with your son. Are there patterns? Can you demonstrate an ability to play different roles in different settings depending on the need? All too often we see the world through present circumstances but reflecting on the past helps you see options for the future.

Chapter Seven
Know Your Position (and Another) Actions
So often, we talk about being great team members or building high performing teams. But few people take the requisite steps to deliver on that promise. As part of sports team, your children have no choice but to immerse themselves in team dynamics. Knowing their

position, and then another, ensures top performance. It's just part of the job. Even if the team isn't exceptional, there are lessons to be gleaned from daily participation. Here are some ways to identify and embrace these key behaviors.

1. Clarify two things: What position is your child playing and what position does she want to be playing? Are they the same? Are they different? It's important to have clarity on the role so it can be studied. If the position being played is different than the preferred position, that may not be such a bad thing, and we'll get to that momentarily. But know the answer to these two questions.

2. Study the position your child is playing carefully and completely, and help them do the same. Understand what is expected in terms of skills, tactics and approaches to the position. How does it most often help a team? How does it most often hurt a team? Help your child become a practitioner.

3. After your child has studied and learned the specifics of her position, have her learn another. If she came up with two different positions going through the first action, you already know what position to study next – the one she wants to be playing. If she isn't sure what to study, choose a position that she interacts with and on which she is often dependent. Help her learn that one.

4. Develop specific exercises to help your daughter master the various components of positional play. This will be different for every position on every type of team – but there will certainly be physical and mental components. Break them down and ensure your daughter is training each part appropriately.

5. Put it all together. Take a step back and help your daughter appreciate how improving her positional aptitude has improved her overall understanding of the team dynamic. Have her talk to coaches and teammates about it, and suggest she aspire to elevate the team's approach to positional awareness. Everyone that functions better as an individual within the context of the whole will be pushing the team to new heights.

Chapter Eight
Play 90 Minutes (And Expect Extra Time) Actions
Unlike many of the behaviors we've explored, playing ninety minutes translates very directly to the field and has an impact on the outcome of a game. It's also a relatively easy concept to discuss with your child. The challenge comes in translating the life lessons to other disciplines. Use these actions to dive deep into the benefits of playing until the final whistle, regardless of outcome.

1. Talk about when the game ends. Seriously, does your child understand the rules of the game? It may seem rudimentary but unless they have a complete grasp of the box within which they're working, it's impossible to play on the edges or even move outside the box in any capacity. This is true in other facets of life as well.

2. Explore the benefits of playing to the end, regardless of perceived outcome. Particularly at a young age, it may not be clear how sustained effort can benefit the future. Outline the possibility of a comeback. Give examples.

3. Cross-training doesn't always have to be physical. Build a mental cross-training program for your child so he can truly learn about belief and grit. Identify people that embody such characteristics and explain why they are examples of these qualities.

4. Incremental improvement is the key to "playing ninety minutes" in a soccer game. Don't start with the end goal, but instead outline a means for your daughter to build up to quality effort for the entire game. Start at forty minutes, then build to sixty minutes, then eighty minutes, and eventually you'll land on ninety minutes or more.

5. Reflect on other areas of life where this concept has meaningful application. It starts with understanding what has meaning to your child – but when you've identified such an area, repeats steps one through four looking at a discipline or activity through that lens. A life lesson to be used anywhere!

Chapter Nine
Play Fast Actions
Everyone admires the naturally fast runners. But speed is about more than innate athletic ability. There are multiple factors that dictate whether you can play fast. There are also benefits that go well beyond beating an opponent. After those elements are understood, it's easier for you and your child to embrace the importance of playing fast as a life lesson. Here are some actions to reinforce this critical concept.

1. Redefine "fast" so that your child understands the expanded concept to include both physical and mental attributes. Only this more sophisticated understanding of "fast" can lead to a full appreciation of its benefits, and an awareness of how speed affects outcomes on the field.

2. Explore how different people achieve speed. Who is leveraging physical tools and who is leveraging mental tools? Are there clear examples of individuals who have mastered both?

3. Identify where your child is most naturally capable of playing fast. Accentuate those abilities and ensure they grow to become a clear strength. Then look at the area where speed is not a strength and talk about why. If your daughter runs fast but isn't situationally prepared, the first step towards improvement is building awareness.

4. Develop a plan to improve on "speed of play." Come up with a running routine and talk chalk. Take a balanced approach and revisit the chapter on making mistakes. Understanding that playing at speed will cause mistakes is critical to development.

5. Repeat steps one through four as it relates to math, art, cooking or music. Where can "playing fast" improve outcomes? How will failing fast improve overall growth?

Chapter Ten
Want the Ball Actions
As a coach or parent, we often assume, erroneously, that kids are just born with the desire to "want the ball" or not. Sure, some kids are more intrinsically capable of embracing this role. But, these qualities can be cultivated in young athletes. Give your athlete various scenarios to consider and explore and watch them want the ball more as time goes on.

1. Contextualize the importance of wanting the ball for the right reasons. If your child is more prone to be a team player, it may be hard for her to break free of selfless habits. Praise that mentality but be sure to explain when "selfishness" is also better for the team. Appeal to selfless behavior to bring out individuality.

2. Study specific actions in your athlete's sport that exemplify individual excellence, in the right context. On a soccer field,

it's not dribbling fifty yards for no reason, ignoring open teammates the whole way, just to lose the ball at the end of your run. It is taking a difficult shot, when your team is down by a goal and it's the best opportunity you've had to score. These situations may be out of character, but they can generate positive outcomes for the team.

3. Explain the extended benefits of maximizing individual opportunities. Talk about how showing courage and confidence can demonstrate leadership. Explore how leadership qualities attained this way ultimately improve the overall team dynamic.

4. Encourage your young athlete to embrace these opportunities, even in the face of "failure," and explain how the upside is far greater than the downside. Fall back on applauding and praising drive and passion, not outcomes. Revisit fun and talk about how enjoyable these competitive situations can be.

5. Regularly examine where wanting the ball is appropriate in other life scenarios – from school to theater to social situations and beyond. What are the equivalent actions of taking a shot late in the game when your team is behind? How do these situations help your child's "team" of choice?

Chapter Eleven
Talk. Then Talk More! Actions
Coaches develop drills that require communication and you can do the same in everyday life. This will reinforce those key behaviors at home with your young athlete. These behaviors, exhibited daily, can get your team working like a fluid and dynamic soccer team. You're also using them off the field. Short bursts of communication geared towards solving problems will become a valuable tool for your child.

1. Discuss in detail why on-field communication is important. Make sure your child knows that it's ok to be the one to talk, even when others aren't. Emphasizing the value of communication – and specifically asking your child to consider how gaining information helps them – will reinforce why it is such a critical asset.

2. Encourage your child to talk to her teammates off the field as well. The more she does, the more natural it will feel to talk while playing. This is true in other facets of life. If you communicate in low-stakes scenarios, you'll be comfortable doing so in high-stakes scenarios as well.

3. Emphasize the power of listening. This will help you build a vocabulary around chosen areas of interest. Know the right terms to use on a soccer field. Likewise, learn terminology to use around the classroom, the house, the library or anywhere else you interact with others who can impact your performance. .

4. Talk about talking. That's right, when you sense that communication can help a group to function well, explore better ways to execute. Speak with your child and encourage him to talk to their teammates about the importance of communication.

5. Model this at home. Review family activities and make sure communication is embedded in them. Whether it's making dinner or cleaning the living room, modeling the usefulness of talking and listening is important to modelling it in behavior.

Chapter Twelve
Know Your Bias Actions
Understanding the role of bias, and then figuring out how to suppress it for some level of objectivity, is a prime example. The following actions will help you embrace this concept.

1. Recognize, as a parent, when you're the most biased. Partiality creeps into the equation often, and it will happen to you. Note your challenges the way that most makes sense for you. If that means writing it down, take that step.

2. Talk to your child about where bias – yours and theirs – can creep in, and why it's valuable to rely on fact and objectivity. The more your child knows about the bias you are trying to overcome, to help him improve, the more you can be aligned towards an outcome.

3. Become the best possible objective observer and encourage your child to do the same. This is the only way you can truly collect helpful data. As parents of youth athletes, we tend have tunnel-vision, and watch only the exploits of our children. Start watching other athletes so you can objectively present your child with data-driven findings of his performance versus others.

4. Leverage inquiry to help your child correlate actions to outcomes. They are on the inside – attending practice every day and listening to a coach's feedback. Your opinion is just that, your opinion. So, when they ask for it, push them to look inward and truly scrutinize the situation from all angles.

5. Ask your child to give you the same type of objective information as you navigate your life. Having them suppress their own bias (yes, kids are biased about their parents as well) to collect data and help you correlate actions to

outcomes will make them better at seeing their own opportunities for growth.

Chapter Thirteen
Good Coaches, Bad Coaches Actions
Of all the anecdotal discussions in this book, the impact of a bad coach is one to which almost everyone can relate. It's also one of the most debilitating scenarios that a sports family can face. The young athlete feels defeated when they are beat down by a bad coach. And parents often feel helpless. In the next chapter we'll explore when it's time to bust through that helpless feeling. But for now, here are some positive actions that can help keep good coaches and bad coaches in perspective.

1. Discuss what really makes a good coach and bad coach so that your young athlete has a clear archetype of each in his mind. Sometimes, a child reacts emotionally to a certain style of coaching. A good coach can feel like a bad coach, and vice versa. The more thoughtful your son's evaluation of the player/coach relationship, the better his judgment will be.

2. Reinforce that all coaches have value, no matter how a player ultimately feels about them. Tune your ear to openly hear critique and assess its value. Coaches always provide another viewpoint for objective feedback.

3. Have your son write down the reasons for playing sports and be sure to read those reasons every time he encounters a bad coach. Make those reasons the focus and control internal variables.

4. Actively seek other voices in a bad coach situation. That may mean that your son spends more time with an assistant coach, outside trainer or knowledgeable parent. Be honest

with that person about the situation – that your son is struggling to connect with a coach – so they understand that you are looking for something different.

5. Try to make it better. That's right, sometimes a bad coach isn't a bad coach at all Instead, the relationship could reflect your own actions. If you feel like the relationship has soured, ask yourself "What can I do to make this better?"

Chapter Fourteen
Best Situation Actions
Society has obfuscated the concept of quitting. A stigma has been attached to those that walk away from something, particularly in sports. To be sure, there are quitters. People that simply don't want to do the work, and then choose to walk away instead. But, that's not what we're talking about here. Instead, we are encouraging a methodical approach to decision-making – specifically choosing to walk away from a bad situation and walk towards a better one. The following five actions will reinforce examination and exploration of the best situation.

1. Define the values that drive youth athletics for your child. In this chapter, we use fun and team cultural elements as key drivers in Kendall's story. But every athlete has a different reason for playing. Know your child's reason and make sure to evaluate the situation against those values.

2. Describe what good looks like, then describe what the best situation looks like. It's easy to react emotionally to a difficult situation – bad coach, bad teammates, etc. – but comparing that scenario to your definition of "good" or "best" can be enlightening. Things may not be as bad as they seem, particularly by your personal standards.

3. Give it time, but a specific amount of time. Many good situations seem bad at the outset. If you completed action number two, and still conclude you truly are not in a good or the best situation, settle on that conclusion then "sleep on it" as they say. Maybe for a week, a month or two months. But give it time to ensure you aren't walking away before improvement can occur.

4. Actively talk to athletes on other teams, at other clubs and beyond. Ask them about their situation. Gauge how a situation fits your values based on those conversations before you choose a new club or team. Do your research so you don't find yourself back in a bad situation again.

5. Define the best situation for other aspects of your life – school, career aspirations, social life, etc. Write this down and return to it anytime you feel like you've deviated from a path of excellence. Sports can teach you that the best situation stimulates growth specific to, and unrelated to a craft.

Chapter Fifteen
More than Soccer Actions
How do you maximize participation in youth sports? By focusing on other things. Not while your child is on the field, but with the countless hours dedicated to sports elsewhere – in the car, at home, etc. Explore the actions below to make sure you're getting more than soccer out of your child's participation in soccer.

1. Use this book to emphasize the life lessons your family can take away from youth sports participation. If you actively prioritize the non-sports values of sports, the lessons become clearer to everyone.

2. Detail the fringe benefits of sports. Kendall wanted to use sports to travel. If soccer or other sports affords this opportunity, consider taking the whole family on soccer trips. Experience new cultures and then talk about them as a family. Make sure you learn along the way. Becoming more cultured and educated because you daughter can kick a soccer ball is awesome.

3. Make a list of topics you want to explore with your child – school, hobbies, etc. – and make them a priority during your drive to and from the field. This is valuable talk time. Use it to the fullest.

4. Explore stretch goals. Your son spent six hours a day in school, two hours playing soccer and another two hours doing homework. There's still time to start a side business, if that's a stretch goal interest. Shift the car ride conversations to business planning and you're well on your way.

5. Don't take any of it too seriously. Chapter One is about ensuring "fun" is part of the equation. When all is said and done, we should find the fun in everything we do. Find a smile or laugh in every soccer situation because, well, there's more to life than soccer.

Chapter Sixteen
Better than You Actions
Are your kids better than you at sports? Before you answer, it's critical to know exactly what that means. How do you define "better?" Is it the skills, the experience, the outcome or something else? In this chapter, we've reviewed how to let your child determine their relationship with sports, then allowing them to develop it exclusively on their terms. That should make them happy and fulfilled in ways you never experienced. Here are some actions to

help reach that point.

1. Other books will tell you to set goals with your son regarding his participation in sports. We're doing the same thing, but without focusing on the individual or team success on the field. Instead, identify the macro-level goals for your son – does he want to play just a few years, casually, competitively, etc. Or is he looking to use sports to improve other aspects of his life? Whatever the goal, make sure you define it. Then revisit it and refine it, ensuring that he controls his relationship with those goals.

2. Actively define all the outcomes related to those goals and choose which will make your child happiest. Work towards happiness as the ultimate outcome, which may bring the value of other activities and benefits into focus.

3. Share your own sports stories with your child. Focus on the things that went poorly and talk about how you wish you had managed your relationship with youth sports differently. Showing vulnerability through your previous experiences will make it easier for your child to share his true goals.

4. Carry the three steps above into other aspects of your child's life. How can he be better than you in every aspect of what he does?

5. Repeatedly question whether you're putting too much value on the outcomes of your son's activities. Is that conducive to him having better experiences than you had? It's not about you, it's about your child.

Resources and
Suggested Reading

Angela Duckworth, *Grit: The Power of Passion and Perseverance* (New York: Scribner, 2016)

Chip Heath and Dan Heath. *The Power of Moments: Why Certain Experiences Have Extraordinary Impact* (New York: Simon & Schuster, 2017)

Daniel Coyle, *The Talent Code: Greatness Isn't Born. It's Grown. Here's How.* (New York: Bantam, 2009)

Daniel Coyle, *The Culture Code: The Secrets of Highly Successful Groups* (New York: Bantam, 2018)

Jeff Haden, *The Motivation Myth: How High Achievers Really Set Themselves Up to Win* (New York: Portfolio, 2018)

John O'Sullivan, *Changing the Game: The Parent's Guide to Raising Happy, High Performing Athletes, and Giving Youth Sports Back to our Kids* (New York: Morgan James Publishing, 2014)

Jon Acuff, *Finish: Give Yourself the Gift of Done* (New York: Portfolio, 2017)

Koppelman, Brian. (Producer). *The Moment with Brian Koppelman* [Audio podcast]. Retrieved from https://itunes.apple.com/us/podcast/the-moment-with-brian-koppelman/id814550071?mt=2

Seth Godin, *The Dip: A Little Book That Teaches You When to Quit (and When to Stick)* (New York: Portfolio, 2007)

About the Author:
Kent Malmros

Kent Malmros holds a B.A. in American History from the University of Pennsylvania, where he graduated Cum Laude.

During his time in Philadelphia, he was both the Sports Editor and Executive Editor at *The Daily Pennsylvanian*, the University's independent student newspaper. Kent was also a member of the Sphinx Senior Honor Society and recipient of the Alumni Association Award of Merit.

After graduation, he began working in software product development and quickly established himself as one of the leading experts in corporate learning technology. He also continued work as part-time journalist for nearly a decade. His writing credits include *The Philadelphia Daily News*, *The Doylestown Intelligencer. The Gazette*, *MLB.com* and *MiLB.com*. Kent worked briefly as a broadcast sports journalist, hosting *The Daily Rewind* on MLB.TV and various radio talk shows for MLB.com. Other on-air work included fill-in sportscasts for WZBN-TV and radio broadcast for the Trenton Titans, a minor league hockey team.

He currently lives in New Hope, Pennsylvania with his wife, Cindy, and two daughters, Kendall and Hayden.

36890217R00150

Made in the USA
Columbia, SC
27 November 2018